# AMERICAN HIRO

## THE ADVENTURES OF BENIHANA'S ROCKY AOKI AND HOW HE BUILT A LEGACY

## JACK McCALLUM

### FOREWORD BY STEVE AOKI

DIVERSION
BOOKS

Diversion Books
A division of Diversion Publishing Corp.
www.diversionbooks.com

First Diversion Books edition, May 2022
Paperback ISBN:  9781635767698
eBook ISBN:  9781635767711

Printed in the United States of America
1  3  5  7  9  10  8  6  4  2

Library of Congress cataloging-in-publication data is available on file

# CONTENTS

# FOREWORD

BY STEVE AOKI, 2021

**M**y father, Rocky Aoki, stood five feet four inches tall but cast a long, long shadow. That's the simplest thing I can say to describe a sometimes difficult, sometimes compassionate, all-times passionate, all-times complicated relationship with this unique man who crammed a hundred years of living into his sixty-nine years on earth.

There were so many dimensions to my father that it's impossible to get him down all at once, which is why I have talked about him in my book, *Blue: The Color of Noise*, and in the Netflix documentary about my life, *I'll Sleep When I'm Dead*. But let me suggest these as the main thematic questions for this foreword: *What were the lessons he taught me and how did he teach them?*

Looking into the Aoki family dynamic through a long lens, one might assume that the child of a man like Rocky, who made lots of money and lived a jet-set lifestyle, would follow that same path. Nothing could be further from the truth. My father didn't want us—and I include my six brothers and sisters here—to grow up with our hands out. If existence was a game of *Who Wants to Be a Millionaire?* my father was definitely not a lifeline, but he was consistent with one piece of advice: *Work ethic is the number one thing on the planet.*

Does a kid always want to hear that? Of course not. But I see now that his version of tough love was incredibly beneficial to me. I learned how to deal with hardship, to brush the dirt off my knees and elbows when I got knocked down, and to get the hell back up. It gave me a certain grit, and I attribute a lot of my success to that.

I did my dutiful stint at Benihana, working in restaurants in Dallas and Oahu under the watchful eye of my older brother, Kevin, the obvious heir to the restaurant throne. So why didn't I live out my life in front of a teppanyaki grill? I have two words: Onion Boy. Kevin had me peeling onions, five hours a day, and I smelled like onions for weeks. The Onion Volcano at Benihana? Don't order it around me.

My father didn't push Benihana down my throat. He wanted the best people to be working there, people who *wanted* to be there, and that was not me. That was okay. My father just wanted me to be great at something. While he didn't always understand my path and my passion for music, there were moments of true connection between us, and they have become even more significant since his death. He came to a couple of my shows in New York City, and it's impossible to express how important that was to me.

When I was at UC-Santa Barbara I wrote an impassioned article in the college newspaper about a fight for ethnic studies. I had forgotten about it until a couple years later when I visited my father. He had that newspaper story framed and hanging on the wall in his home office. I could not believe it. Did he care about the politics of ethnic studies? Did he even read the article? I'm not sure, but that's not the point. The point is that he was proud of his son—*me*—for having accomplished something.

Though I emphasize that my father never helped me financially, in a more important way he actually spoiled me. I was spoiled with *experiences*. Traveling the world with my father, watching him interact with people famous and ordinary, observing up close his balls-out sense of adventure, and having a larger-than-life personality to live up to had a profound effect on me and the formation of my character.

You can't add them and come up with a figure on a ledger, but they're more real than cash.

Another advantage I had was my mother, Chizuru. Whatever doubts she might have felt about my career path and the way I was walking it, she was always behind me. My mother was a nurturer, a fellow visionary, a believer in my potential. She's my heart and my soul—and sometimes she was even my bank. Mom bought me my first car, an Isuzu Rodeo. At seven grand it was a steal, which is appropriate because it actually *had* been stolen. We got it at a police auction. On another occasion early in my business career, I had run out of money to meet what was then a very modest payroll. My dad could have probably found the cash wedged between the seat cushions of any number of his luxury cars, but it was Mom who went into her savings and got the ten grand. Though I'm sure they never saw it this way, one could apply to my parents the ancient Chinese concept of duality—yin and yang.

Yin and yang was kind of how I saw my father. True, he was the glitzy, Americanized entrepreneur, but he was also the archetypal Japanese man: aware of manners, selfless, restrained, and preoccupied with self-sustenance. That dual character, that ability to inhabit two worlds and be of two cultures, was a magnet that drew people to him.

Many people knew my father, or thought they knew him, or talked about knowing him, but there's one quality a lot of people miss—his compassion and his generosity. That was the wellspring of his business. He honestly wanted people to be happy, to have a good time, to be among one another and enjoying life. He never stopped wanting that.

My family had some messy moments that you'll read about in this book. After my father married his third wife, Keiko, she made it difficult for us to be together as a family. But as my father's condition worsened, we came together. I'll describe my own final moments with my father in one of the closing chapters, but I will share this with you: He didn't think he was going to die. His belief in himself was as indomitable as it had always been, as strong as it was when he bet his life on the novel concept that Americans would like to sit together and eat and be entertained, as strong as it was when he strapped himself into a powerboat or a hot-air balloon and took off into the wild blue yonder.

He was my drive, my ambition, my fuel. Whatever else I am, I am my father's son.

*Steven Aoki is a Grammy-nominated producer, a Billboard Award–winning deejay, an author, a philanthropist, and one of the world's best-known figures in electronic music. The son of Rocky and Chizuru Aoki, he founded Dim Mak Records in 1996, when he was just nineteen.*

# INTRODUCTION

In the dining room of the twenty-nine-room Aoki house in Tenafly, New Jersey, there sits a lovely wire cage, home for the family's four lovebirds. Three of them make a lot of noise but seem content with their lot in the cage. The fourth doesn't squawk much, but he's constantly escaping from the cage and looking for a way to get out of the house. No one can figure out how he does it. A close inspection of the cage reveals no obvious exits. And if it's so easy, why don't the other birds do it?

"I guess he's a Houdini," said Rocky Aoki.

And so is Rocky Aoki. Of the four sons of Yunosuke and Katsu Aoki, the eldest—named Hiroaki, which was later changed for American convenience to Rocky—is the one who left the cage and made like Houdini. In his forty-six years (he turns forty-seven in October 1985) he has pulled all kinds of rabbits out of all kinds of hats. He built his multimillion-dollar Benihana restaurant empire from one hole-in-the-wall site in New York City. Though never a swimmer, he became a top offshore powerboat racer. Though he feared heights, he made a record 6,000-mile flight in a gas balloon. Though never a navigator, he's currently involved in a project that would take him 3,000 feet underwater in a unique two-man submersible, and he dreams of winning the America's Cup for his native land.

He plays the way he works—hard and often, joyfully and to the hilt. And he has paid for it. An ugly zipper scar runs the length of his chest, the legacy of a gruesome 1979 boating accident in San Francisco Bay that by rights should have killed him. Dozens of other scars crisscross his legs, the result of two other accidents that finally forced him to retire from active competition in 1982. But wait! At the 1984 world championships in Key West, Rocky (unbeknownst to most of the boating world as well as his own family) climbed back in and navigated for eventual champion Al Copeland. Though everyone has advised him against it, and though it takes him 10 minutes to get moving in the morning because of the damage the wrecks have done to his legs, Rocky is again thinking about getting behind the wheel of a powerboat.

No Japanese of note has more easily made the transition to America than Rocky. Everything that made Japan Japan—the ancient traditions, the courtly manners, the seniority system that reveres the old, the stoic response to life—was anathema to Rocky. These were reasons to get out of Japan and get to America. Yet there are things about him that are uniquely Asian: his reticence in crowds and his almost serene response to the pressures on him every day. He straddles two worlds, two cultures, two styles. Not surprisingly, back in his native Japan, people are of two minds about Rocky Aoki. To the young, non-traditional Japanese, he's a folk hero; to the older, more conservative generations, he's an enigma at best. In this country his status is more secure. He's an American hero.

Jack McCallum
November 25, 1984

*The Introduction and Chapters 1 through 13 comprise the original 1985 edition of this book. Chapter 15 and the epilogue have been included for this 2022 edition.*

# CHAPTER

It didn't take long for a young wrestler named Hiroaki Aoki to lose his given Japanese name once he stepped off the plane at New York City's Idlewild Airport in June 1959. "What's your name, son?" a member of the Amateur Athletic Union, the American group sponsoring the series of exhibitions between the Japanese and the Americans, asked the nineteen-year-old Aoki. "Hiroaki Aoki," said the young man proudly. It was a good name, a noble-sounding name, as Aoki's father, Yunosuke, knew when he gave it to him. "Aoki Hiroaki," Yunosuke used to say in an official tone. "General Aoki Hiroaki!" It is the Japanese custom to say the last name first, and Yunosuke, befitting the samurai strain of his ancestry, thought the harsh, snappish quality to the name sounded properly military.

But "Aoki Hiroaki" or "Hiroaki Aoki" didn't last long once the young Aoki touched on the shores of America. "I don't understand 'Hiroaki,'" said the AAU representative. "It sounds like Rocky. Let's call you 'Rocky.'" And Rocky it was—then, now, and forevermore.

"Rocky Aoki" was a match made in nomenclature heaven. If the Italians can lay first claim to Rocky, from their proper name of Rocco, it is the Americans who have taken it over and stamped a Rocky as an American type. Tough, hard, peppery, resilient, eager, energetic. Name your adjective, but this young Japanese fit into the nickname as easily as his tiny (5 feet, 4 inches; 114 pounds), smoothly muscled frame fit into his wrestling uniform.

It might have galled another Japanese—or a young man from any culture for that matter—to so easily lose a part of his heritage, but Aoki Hiroaki loved the name Rocky. He had an innate feeling that it would be good for him, that it could make him stand out amid a sea of unpronounceable Asian monikers, and Rocky Aoki, even at this age, was not radically opposed to anything that could make him stand out. Besides, it was an *American* name, and Rocky, more than any of his teammates, loved almost anything American.

"From the first moment I met him, Rocky was different than most of the Japanese boys," said John Mandel, the wrestling chairman of the AAU. "Heck, he was more American than I was. He didn't follow the rules; he didn't toe the line, like most of the Japanese kids. That didn't mean he didn't work hard, because he did. But he just did it his own way. He did what the hell he wanted to."

Mandel had seen a lot of the world when he first laid eyes on Rocky Aoki twenty-five years ago, yet he remains captivated by the moment. "He was *different*," says Mandel. "That's the only way I can describe it. *Different*."

That Rocky Aoki could impress a man like Mandel *before* he made his millions says something about the eldest son of Yunosuke and Katsu Aoki. Mandel, still a burly bear of a man at age sixty-eight, must have been something to look at back in 1959. Some years earlier he had been one of five men interviewed to portray Tarzan, eventually losing the role to Buster Crabbe. Add to that fact Mandel's vocation as a New York City detective and there emerges a portrait of a man who could be quite selective in whom he's impressed by. Yet the newly christened Rocky was something special to Mandel, who would more or less adopt him one year later.

Actually, Mandel had been on the lookout for the young Aoki. On an earlier trip to Japan, Mandel had met Yunosuke Aoki; they had a mutual friend in Ichiro Hatta, the head of the Japanese Wrestling Federation. "Keep your eye out for my boy," Mr. Aoki had told Mandel. "He wants to go to school in the United States, and maybe you could get him a scholarship." Such arrangements were Mandel's specialty; after all, he had gotten one Japanese wrestler an assistant coaching job at, of all places, West Point.

Mandel had been intrigued by Rocky's father, who seemed an unusually buoyant gentleman, a pole apart from the traditionally reserved Japanese men he was used to dealing with. And very few Americans knew the Japanese as well as Mandel. As early as 1951, just ten years after the bombing of Pearl Harbor, Mandel had fought through a lot of quasi-patriotic resistance to arrange a series of exhibitions in the United States between the Japanese and the American teams. It was a combination of Yunosuke Aoki's request and Mandel's fascination with Rocky's instinctually Americanized ways that brought Mandel and Rocky together.

But what made Rocky the way he was? What forces conspired to form the Americanized Japanese, the eager expatriate? "That's hard to say," says Mandel. "That's just the way he was, that's all." It *is* hard to say, but the importance of two major factors can hardly be ignored— the strong personality of his late father and the transitional nature of the Japan in which he was reared.

Hiroaki Aoki, the first child of Yunosuke and Katsu Aoki, was born on October 9, 1938, into a society locked in turmoil between a kind of placid prosperity and a restless militarism. Befitting their prosperity, Yunosuke owned, at the time of Rocky's birth, a jazz coffee shop called Ellington, so named for the American musician. Befitting the movement toward militarism, the Japanese captured the key Chinese province of Canton shortly after Rocky's birth. Just three years later, of course, the trend toward militarism would be complete with the bombing of Pearl Harbor, and Mr. Aoki's Americanized coffee shop was no more.

The militaristic bent of the Japanese is perhaps more easily comprehensible, at least to the Western mind, than the easy-going, prosperous age that preceded it. To the Western world, there has always been something vaguely warlike about the Japanese, a combination, no doubt, of unreal prejudice and the very real December 7 attack over the Hawaiian skies. But before all that, back in the 1920s, Japan was actually reveling in what American historian Edwin O. Reischauer called "the Japanese variant of the flapper and jazz age." There were many reasons for the prosperity, but the primary one was economic: The European powers, by becoming involved in World War I, "had left their Asian markets to Japan," according to Reischauer, and the Japanese had taken advantage. The influx of liberalizing ideas from the victors of World War I, primarily the United States, made their influence felt, too, so that the Japanese knew the tools of the Western devil and had the means to buy them.

At home in this milieu was one Yunosuke Aoki, the son of middle-class parents from the prefecture of Wakayama, about 150 miles west of Tokyo. Yunosuke's family descended from the *bushi* class, the samurai, the warrior-administrators. A century earlier the samurai class was situated at the top of the extremely stratified Japanese society, and Yunosuke, like others of his generation, still felt the subtle tugs and pulls of his ancient lineage; arguably, Yunosuke's generation, the last to be educated without a pervasive American influence, was also the last to feel strongly the traditional class distinctions. But at the same time Yunosuke was a thoroughly modern man long removed from the samurais, and so did he follow his instincts and made his way to the big city of Tokyo when he came of age.

Hiroaki Aoki got his build from his father. Yunosuke was a small, wiry man, a shade shorter than Rocky but capable of the same quick, athletic movements. His son would later translate those movements into athleticism; Yunosuke turned them into dance. Nothing reflected the influx of Western ideas into Japan more than popular culture, which, for a period, turned its back on its more traditional forms, like the elaborate, sentimental Kabuki theater, in favor of American and European influences. Yunosuke Aoki spent most of his free time studying the moves of Fred Astaire, the American dancer being among the most popular of the movie heroes imported by Japan. Yunosuke was an actor and a choreographer in Tokyo stage productions, and eventually he gained his greatest fame as a tap dancer in a form of Japanese vaudeville that was much like our own, using the stage name of Hiroyuki Go, pronounced "goo." Rocky, in fact, remembers his father talking about performing with a strip teaser in his early days. Employing his celebrity status, Mr. Aoki in 1932 opened a tap dance studio called the Hiroyuki Go Tap Dance Institute, the first of many enterprises.

One of Yunosuke's brightest students was a young girl from the small town of Tatsuishi in Gumma, a prefecture about sixty miles from Tokyo. Katsu Hosono, exactly nine years Yunosuke's junior (they were both born on September 25), was a bright, vibrant young woman with theatrical aspirations. Just getting out of her small town, where her parents were farmers, had been a grand aspiration in itself. "Not too many young girls did that in those days," says Mrs. Aoki, who is still active in her family's Japan operation.

The day after her high school graduation, the seventeen-year-old Miss Hosono arrived in Toyko against the wishes of her father. Her vocational plans were at that time unfocused: "I just wanted to spend my life there." She visited employment agencies every day for a month until she landed a job as an office clerk at a small newspaper company specializing in entertainment news. Japan was a relentlessly macho society in those days (and still is in many ways), and Miss Hosono was forced to quit when her boss wouldn't leave her alone after hours. She got a different job at a publishing company, and the same thing happened. She had beauty, grace, charm, and no thought of selling herself. She explains her feelings to a translator, her words coming through lyrically.

"Before I came to Tokyo, I heard Tokyo is a scary city, and I really thought it was true from these scary two experiences. I was crying for loneliness and poorness those days."

Things took a turn the other way when she landed a job as a dancer at a Tokyo social club, an entirely respectable job in those days, the sleazy New York version notwithstanding. The tango was her specialty. Through an acquaintance at the club she met a vaudevillian named Korema Arima, who suggested she take tap dance lessons in an effort to become a stage dancer, a secret ambition of hers. The best studio around was run by the noted popular hoofer, Hiroyuki Go.

Katsu didn't have enough money to pay for her lessons, so she did extra work in the Aoki household such as cleaning and laundering. Though Katsu described him as "a very strict teacher," their tutor-tyro relationship soon blossomed into something else, and within a year of meeting this bright, young, vibrant woman, Yunosuke married her.

"It was not a difficult decision at all when I gave up my career for marriage, because I knew I really didn't have the talent to be a successful dancer," said Katsu.

Still, it took a woman of unusual courage and determination to leave her farm for the big city. And even from a distance, it's easy to have a sense of the personal dynamism of Yunosuke Aoki, descended from samurai but tap-tap-tapping away in the modern world. It's no mystery that their union produced someone like Hiroaki "Rocky" Aoki. Their other children were Yasuhiro, born on November 7, 1939, Hiromitsu, born on March 22, 1941, and Shiro, born on October 10, 1943. Yasuhiro died of a collapsed lung on April 30, 1983, but the other two brothers are both thriving in the restaurant business. Hiro owns two Japanese restaurants called Robata of Japan in the St. Louis area, while Shiro owns three restaurants in upstate New York (where he lives) and two in Denver, Colorado, all of them called Gasho.

Business was brisk at Ellington, remembers Mrs. Aoki. "When we opened the teahouse [in 1935], people had a longing for American culture and the country. The idea to use American jazz worked out very good for us."

The war ended all that. Rocky was only four years old when American B-29s rained their bombs on Tokyo, but he can remember the fear and the confusion. There was little time for preoccupation—everyone joined in the war effort. His father had gotten a deferment because he was an entertainer—an ironic twist for a samurai descendant. Nevertheless he performed a military obligation, which in his case was polishing Japanese fighter planes at a military works factory. "The kind that bombed Pearl Harbor," says his eldest son today, a small smile on his face. "That's how it was then," says Rocky. "'People in America cannot appreciate what it's like to have the war fought in their own country. If you had gold teeth, then you were supposed to take them out and give them to the government so they could melt them down. I remember I had a little dog at the time. I had to give it away so the army could kill it and use the skin for the lining of a hat."

The Aoki family suffered neither more nor less than most Japanese families in Tokyo. B-29s flew over daily while the citizens went through their obligatory civil defense drills. At times they got along for days without water, and the only food available in quantity was potatoes and noodles. One of Mrs. Aoki's clearest memories is watching her children and her neighbors' children losing weight. The Aokis procured food in two principal ways: Yunosuke got it on the black market, having been familiar with it during his operation of Ellington, and Katsu traded her kimonos for it.

Early in 1944 the family decided to play it safe and move to a less evident target—Katsu's native province of Gumma, where they took up residence with her family. Life there wasn't easy—"It was pretty odd living with a farmer and not being able to get vegetables because we had to give them to the government," remembers Rocky—but things were not so bad that Rocky's family had to join their neighbors in butchering and eating a stray horse killed by an American bomb.

Rocky did not fully grasp the significance, but he clearly remembers his family and dozens of neighbors sitting around a communal radio listening to Emperor Hirohito ask his people to "bear the unbearable" and give up the fight. The date was August 15, at noon, and many of the Japanese, wearing ceremonial kimonos, were listening to the voice of their emperor for the first time. Out in the province of Gumma they had had only sketchy reports of the destruction of Hiroshima and Nagasaki, but there was no mistaking the urgent tone in Hirohito's voice. There was no hope. "It was lost on me," remembers Rocky, "but everybody else was crying and moaning." On September 2, the Japanese representative aboard the U.S.S. *Missouri*, anchored in Tokyo Bay, signed the surrender papers. Back in Gumma, the citizens prepared for what would certainly be a raping and plundering spree by American soldiers. Rocky remembers sitting on his couch and fashioning crude bamboo arrows to protect himself and his family.

"It may seem hard to believe that a nation the size of California thought we could beat the entire United States," says Rocky today, "but we did. To the people of Japan, it was a defeat, a tragic defeat."

But not a fatal one. Historically, the Japanese, in the words of former RAND Corporation researcher Paul F. Langer, "have never resisted foreign influences as stubbornly as other Asian nations." Is that a weakness, a sign of weak-willed obsequiousness? Or is it a strength, emblematic of a certain pragmatism that, in the long run at least, has paid dividends for the Westernized economic power that is contemporary Japan? A little of both, probably, but in the coming years Hiroaki Aoki would have that quality of adaptability in spades.

Seven-year-old Hiroaki Aoki had little sense of his country's desperate situation at the war's end. About 2 million Japanese had been killed, several more million were incapacitated (due to injuries and illness), and about 10 million were homeless; in Tokyo alone, two thirds of the population had lost its housing, including the Aokis, who found that their old home had been destroyed. All he remembers is how everyone went to work. "Sixteen hours a day, six days a week," says Rocky. "It's not surprising to me how they became a world power when you see how we went to work."

One of those was Yunosuke Aoki. By the time the war started, his hoofing days had pretty much ended—he had found that running a coffee shop was a much easier way to make a living—but he would have had to abandon the theater anyway because it simply didn't exist in the years immediately following the war. There was a country to be rebuilt.

Mr. Aoki's Ellington had been located in a central area of Tokyo known as Nihonbashi, the financial district, and it was to there that he returned after bringing his family back to Tokyo late in 1945. There was no possibility of reopening a club with the same name—though the United States had Japan in a virtual stranglehold in terms of its reconstruction, its leadership expressly forbade any businesses with American names—but Mr. Aoki did hear of an opportunity less than a block away from his old shop, and back into the coffee shop business he went. It was the right business for the right time. The Japanese have always craved coffee, tea, and the sweets that have been traditionally offered at their coffee shops. At the same time the coffee shops have fulfilled a social and very practical need. Housing in Japan has always been a problem—it still is despite today's prosperity—and people have needed places to take their guests because there simply isn't room for entertaining in many homes. For that specific reason, the Kobiyashi family opened a French-style coffee shop called Bon-Bon right after the war; years later in America Rocky Aoki would marry the daughter, Chizuru, from that family.

Mr. Aoki needed a new name for his shop. One day as he explored the ruins of some bombed-out downtown buildings, he found a saffron flower growing amid the destruction. The word next to *saffron* in the Japanese dictionary is *benihana*. Sometimes *benihana* is translated as "red flower," but it literally means "saffron," and thus did the first small link in what would become a multimillion-dollar chain get its name.

Yunosuke and Katsu worked side by side in the shop. Fortunately for them, their strengths complemented each other. "My father was strictly a host type," said Rocky. "He made quite a few mistakes because he wasn't aware of financial matters. But my mother was a born bookkeeper. She knew what to do with it. She knew how to keep it." Even Katsu, upon reflection today, says she never thought of her late husband "as a businessman."

But that generalization can be carried too far; even Rocky, who would later have business disagreements with his father over the running of Benihana in America, finds exceptions to it sometimes. It was basically his father's idea, for example, to serve sugar, real sugar, in that first Benihana. That may not seem particularly noteworthy except that a vast majority of the shops at that time served a sugar substitute because it was much cheaper. Mr. and Mrs. Aoki put the real sugar in bowls, and they put a bowl on each table. Rocky remembers how flabbergasted new customers were when they saw real sugar, and how they ladled teaspoonful after teaspoonful into their coffee or tea. Furthermore, the Aokis used the real sugar to bake their cakes, too, so that the best place to get sweetness and light in Tokyo was at Benihana. The Aokis weren't afraid to go against the restaurant norm, and twenty years later, their eldest son would go against the norm, too, and find success.

That first Benihana had another reason for success—it kept prices in line, despite the exorbitant cost (Rocky estimates that sugar cost as much in war-ravaged Japan forty years ago as it does in America today). That was no accident. Rocky remembers his father pedaling his *riyaka* (a combination bicycle-wagon) on a 20-mile round trip to buy sugar and rice in 300-pound packages and other restaurant necessities at cheaper prices.

So, consider the different aspects of this Yunosuke Aoki. Unwilling or unable to completely surrender his samurai heritage, he gave his eldest son a general's name. Yet he himself adopted the ways of the West, tap dancing for the masses, stealing the hearts of young girls like Katsu Hosono at his own studio. Almost anyone who ever knew him and his wife placed the more solid business head on her shoulders, yet Yunosuke, too, did whatever he had to do to improve his product and maximize his profit, which included an arduous journey on a bicycle and bartering on the black market. Should there be any surprise when his son evolved into a similarly complex package, some of this and some of that, a pair of tap shoes and a samurai sword?

# CHAPTER

The Japanese have always felt a strong need for an orderly world, and this was reflected in every aspect of society, including family life. The members interacted according to a strict hierarchical order with the father, of course, at the top and the youngest child at the bottom. This was not the casual hierarchy based upon age, which usually springs up in American families, but a highly structured caste system with each family member accepting all the privileges and responsibilities of his or her "rank." In terms of siblings, the eldest son was definitely at the top, harkening back to the feudal days when only the first-born son of the emperor was in the line of succession. The Japanese even have different terms to designate the older and younger brother, *chonan* for the former, *inan* for the latter. According to Langer, the eldest son got a preferred seat at meals, ahead of other children, grandmothers, aunts, and yes, even the mother.

Hiroaki Aoki was *chonan*. It's difficult to say how much that affected the man he eventually became, but in the Aoki household in Japan the sibling life revolved around the eldest, who was an emperor among princes. Symbolically and literally, Rocky's other brothers have spent much of their life trying to catch up to him, and they haven't done it yet.

One of Rocky's clearest memories from his boyhood was the money that flowed into his parents' coffee shop. Neither he nor his mother can remember the exact figures, but Rocky estimates that the first Benihana, in the years around 1950, was grossing the family about $50,000 annually. The net must have been about $15,000, so they were salting away a couple hundred dollars per day. Stuffing away is a more apt description. His parents didn't own a cash register in the early years of the business, and the postwar banking situation was somewhat tenuous, so they simply kept it in their home. Rocky loves to mimic his mother lifting the cash drawer, putting it down, counting the money, and stashing it under the bed. Years later, until Rocky learned something about American banking, he and his mother would do the same thing with the monies from his first New York restaurant.

A few years after the Aokis opened the first Benihana coffeehouse, Mrs. Aoki's niece's husband, who was American, suggested they turn it into a restaurant—continue specializing in the sugary baked goods and sweet coffee but expand the menu. They did, and the restaurant, also called Benihana, was even more successful than the coffeehouse. The business made them a well-to-do, upper-class Japanese family. But though they demanded that their eldest son help out in the shop, they never put it before the value of an education. Perhaps it was a carryover from ancient Japan when the merchant class was considered the lowest rung on the societal ladder, or perhaps the Aokis were just more enlightened on such matters, but Rocky was never given the impression that he was to ignore his own schooling in favor of Learning the Business, the traditional expectation for *chonan*. Tad Suga, who today is vice-president of Benihana International Trading, was raised in Tokyo during the same postwar era as Rocky (at forty-four, he's two years younger), yet his indoctrination was totally different.

"My father was an extremely introverted man," says Suga. "He was very much a traditional Japanese man, involved in spiritual matters, and he just assumed I would take over his job at a small construction company. When I didn't show an interest in that, when my education took me in a different direction, toward restaurant management, he was very upset with me." So upset with Suga, in fact, that he refused to recognize him as a son, the Japanese equivalent of disownment.

Several factors conspired to give a young man like Hiroaki an Americanized education, not the least of which was the fact that, to a large extent, the Americans were doing the teaching. And just about everything else. The dominating personality in Japan in the years immediately following the war was one General Douglas MacArthur, whose official title was the Supreme Commander for the Allied Powers (SCAP), and many of the Japanese looked upon him almost as a god. Whatever MacArthur said, the Japanese (most of them anyway) acceded to, and one of the strongest emphases of Americanization came in the schools. In retrospect, many historians believe the Americanization was too radical, but not many Japanese stopped and thought about it at the time.

In the Aoki household, the eldest son was encouraged to study and to embrace the new ideas disseminated by Japan's conquerors. The prestigious private school, Keio, to which Hiroaki was sent by his parents in the seventh grade, was itself founded by the best-known popularizer of knowledge about the West, a nineteenth-century explorer named Fukuzawa Yukichi. Later, Hiroaki would continue on at Keio University, one of the two or three most prestigious schools in all of Japan. Then, too, it was just not in the makeup of the eldest Aoki son, or most of the Japanese for that matter, to waste a lot of time mourning the loss of the war and muttering under their breaths about the evil Americans. "We just avoided the subject," says Rocky. "I simply can never remember having any resentment about the United States." Historian Langer says it another way in his book *Japan, Yesterday and Today*: ". . . the individual Japanese was not plagued by feelings of personal guilt. He easily convinced himself that during the war he had shouted, 'Down with the United States!' merely because he had been told to do so. Once the fighting was over, the problem, as he saw it, was to rebuild the country rapidly and efficiently."

Hiroaki was a bright boy. To gain entrance to Keio as a fourteen-year-old, he had to pass a rigorous entrance examination, which two of his other brothers, Hiromitsu and Yasuhiro, would later fail. (Shiro passed the exam but attended Keio only briefly.) But Hiroaki was no angel. In American terms, think of him as the quick-thinking, quick-moving, charismatic leader (Russ Tamblyn perhaps) of a fifties street gang, back in the age when such gangs used their fists and their wits instead of weapons and drugs. James Dean would be the wrong image—Rocky was no brooding, sensitive, semi outcast. He was in the thick of things always, a good student who did more than his share of educational underachieving and spent much of his time elbowing his way to the front of extracurricular activities.

"I was always wise guy," says Rocky. It remains one of his favorite words. "Wise guy." His youngest brother, Shiro, the one who would perhaps be the most in awe of Hiroaki's educational and pugilistic prowess, says it another way. "He was a wild man. I mean it, wild. There was always something a little different about him." As when the brothers were playing baseball in a supposedly protected area of the street near their home. When a cabdriver drove through the barriers, young Shiro picked up a stone and heaved it at the cab. The driver took exception, backed up, got out of his car, and grabbed Shiro. Rocky didn't hesitate. He picked up a baseball bat, crept behind the man, and slugged him over the head, knocking him unconscious.

Only Mrs. Aoki's payment of the man's hospital bill saved Rocky from jail. Mrs. Aoki agrees: "He was a born-wild boy."

As the eldest, Rocky perhaps felt the pressure to protect his brothers, but that wasn't the whole story, either. He fought constantly with Yasuhiro and Shiro, and Rocky cannot remember a single instance when it did not end up in an absolute bloodbath. On one occasion Yasuhiro appeared to hold the trump card when he broke a bamboo pole over Rocky's head. Bleeding profusely, Rocky somehow found the strength to knock him out with one punch. Not exactly the stuff that Wally and Beaver were known to do, but then there was no samurai in the Cleaver background. Rocky can remember only one occasion when he decided to get physical with his father, who had scolded him for fighting. He threw a punch at Yunosuke and knocked him backward. The father threw an ashtray back at him and hit him in the chest. End of fight. There's every evidence that Yunosuke was proud of his eldest's spunk, but at the same time the shoving incident drew a hazy battle line in their relationship. Obedient Japanese sons do not throw punches at their fathers, no matter how forward-looking the beliefs of the latter.

Rocky fought at home, in the streets, and in school. When Rocky was sixteen, he walked—or probably strutted—past a group of seedy-looking characters on a Tokyo street corner who offered him some girlie photos for a price. Rocky had other ideas. He swiped the photos from the men, warned them never to return to the corner again, and took off. Later, he found out they were members of the *Yakuza,* the Japanese version of the Mafia, and he could have been killed.

"I knew what I was doing was wrong and it was dangerous," he said, "but it was like I couldn't stop myself from a single challenge. I couldn't sleep for a week after I took those pictures. It wasn't like I did it and forgot about it. I had a brain. I knew the trouble I could get in. But I did it because I loved the fight, the challenge."

Young Hiroaki presented interesting dichotomies. He fought constantly with his father, yet invariably listened to his mother and couldn't bear to defy her. As a young boy he emulated his father's musical abilities and practiced for hours on a bass guitar, even joining at an early age what his mother today terms a "rocken-roll band." Yet once he turned his back on music for athletics in high school, he never looked back at it. He had a good mind, yet he did dumb things, such as stealing girlie photos from organized criminals. His was an entirely proper, upper-middle-class upbringing, yet he loved occasional forays into the demimonde of Tokyo. And though he never appeared to be much interested in the particulars of his parents' restaurant business, he showed an instinctively entrepreneurial sense when he used his dirty pictures to publish a few issues of a quasi-girlie magazine, which he sold around school.

At Keio, Rocky was known as a *bancho*—roughly translated, the chief or leader of a segment of the student body. "We didn't have the chains and the motorcycle thing," remembers Rocky, "but we did do a lot of fighting. And I was like a pit bull, always ready to fight to the last. I remember a doctor at school telling me once, 'Aoki, you should go into the medical field. You're evidently not afraid of blood.'"

Mrs. Aoki, in that time-tested tradition of the mother with the wayward son, was a frequent visitor to Keio School. A list of her son's transgressions would be read to her, though they would usually be tempered by a listing of his intellectual achievements and a statement of his vast potential "if he'd only apply himself." On one occasion he applied himself to becoming Keio's one and only bancho, by answering the request of another bancho to talk things over. The discussion was to take place on a second-floor staircase inside the school, but before it could begin, Rocky pushed the other boy down the stairs. Fortunately, the other boy received only minor injuries; Rocky received a three-month vacation from school, and for that reason one of Keio School's potentially brightest students graduated behind his class.

When Hiroaki wasn't pushing other banchos off staircases or befuddling his teachers, he was competing in athletics. He started out in karate and had moderate success but thought he was too small. He was an outstanding long-distance runner—on one occasion he won a district championship at the half-marathon distance of thirteen miles—but he preferred sports with physical contact. Finally, in his second year of high school at Keio, he discovered wrestling.

It was the ideal sport for a young bancho with Rocky's talents. First, his natural endurance, a Japanese characteristic to begin with, was reinforced by his heritage from a pair of dancers. Second, wrestling (this is the legitimate kind, not the eye-gouging spectacle that runs on late-night television) is an extremely scientific sport, a countermove for every move, and it was a natural for a young man such as Hiroaki, who liked to use his brain at the same time he liked to push opponents off staircases. Third, it had different weight classes, so that an athlete of Aoki's size (he weighed barely ninety pounds when he started wrestling) would not be at a disadvantage. Finally, wrestling is more than anything a test of wills—who will throw in the towel, who will be there at the end—and the eldest son of Yunosuke Aoki was a master at the head game.

The only question was this: Could Hiroaki stop fighting in the street long enough to become a good wrestler?

"I completely stopped fighting the day I became really involved in wrestling," he says. "I dedicated myself totally to it. I just knew it was the sport for me. I knew I could become one of the best at it, and I worked toward that goal. Monday through Friday, three hours a day most of the year, I dedicated myself to wrestling."

And it paid off. He captained the team at Keio and became one of Japan's top lightweights at the age of nineteen. World-class wrestlers frequently don't peak until their mid- or late twenties, and indeed, Rocky had one wrestler he couldn't beat out to gain the first spot on Japan's 1960 Olympic team, but he did make it as an alternate. That earned him passage to America on the fateful 1959 tour. He wrestled fourteen American opponents at his regular 114.5-pound weight and defeated all of them; he lost only once, when he moved up a weight class and was beaten by one of the American Olympians, Dave Auble, who would later be a colleague on the powerboating circuit.

Rocky impressed everyone who met him, both with his wrestling and his outgoing, Americanized personality. When the tour was over, Mandel promised to help him earn a scholarship. "I'll be back," Rocky Aoki told him. "You can bet on that."

The Aoki family in Tokyo; *from right to left,* Katsu (Mama-san), Hiroaki (Rocky), Yasuhiro, Hiromitsu, Shiro, and Yunosuke (Papa-san).

A wrestling champion. Following the 1960 Olympic Games in Rome, Rocky went to New York where, under the aegis of the prestigious NYAC, he won the National AAU championships in 1962, 1963, and 1964.

While at college in New York, Rocky lived alone in a small downtown flat. According to his mother, he called home often but rarely to ask for money. "I think maybe he was lonely and a little bit homesick."

Selling ice cream in Harlem. This is the now-famous truck from which Rocky earned his start-up money for the first Benihana restaurant.

With the ink on his college diploma still drying, Rocky launched himself into seventeen-hour workdays perfecting a new dining concept, which was to revolutionize America's restaurant industry. Said Rocky, "In those days, I had to know every detail of running a restaurant, and I was pretty good at it."

The Benihana dining experience. Rocky's carefully trained Japanese chefs delighted American diners with their ability to entertain as well as prepare delicious meals.

Despite periodic tensions within the Aoki clan, the family took pride in Rocky's rise. Here Rocky, *right*, regales kid brother Shiro, *left*, and Yunosuke (Papa-san) with a humorous anecdote.

"I'm no chef," admitted Rocky, "but I know what I want my guys to do at the Hibachi table, and I know how to teach. Maybe that's enough."

Rocky with actor Sidney Poitier and unidentified friend.

# CHAPTER

**3**

As twenty-one-year-old Rocky Aoki walked through the terminal at Idlewild Airport en route to seeking his fame and fortune in America, he espied a green bill lying under a chair in one of the gate areas. His father had told him America was a land of opportunity "where money can be found anywhere," but this was ridiculous. Relaxing in the sitting room of his mansion in Tenafly, New Jersey, Rocky pantomimes the discovery.

"Here's the bill over here, and I'm walking along, glancing at it, and thinking, 'Money. It's even lying around on the floor. What a place!' If I hadn't been with some other people, I would've picked it up. But I figured I'd see some lying around later." As it turned out, making money wasn't quite that easy, even for Rocky.

The date was August 31, 1960, when Rocky arrived back in the United States to finish his final years of college. His first tour of America as a wrestler was behind him and so was an eventful trip to the Rome Olympics in August. Since the teammate in front of him stayed healthy, alternate Rocky hadn't gotten a chance to wrestle, but he did lead the Japanese team in taking photos. One of his favorite subjects was a brash, young American boxer from Louisville, Kentucky, named Cassius Clay. Just eleven years later Rocky would be promoting one of his heavyweight championship fights in Japan, though Clay didn't remember their first meeting.

Rocky had made a firm decision to come to America even before the Olympics. In fact, he purchased a new Alfa Romeo in Rome and had it shipped directly to America, after which he followed without even returning to Japan.

Rocky's college situation was confused. Mandel had gotten him athletic scholarship offers at C. W. Post College on Long Island, Springfield College in Massachusetts, Michigan State, and Iowa State, all outstanding wrestling schools, yet Rocky held out a hope for Cornell and its influential School of Hotel and Restaurant Management. More accurately, Yunosuke, who was pushing him toward a career in the restaurant business, held out a hope for Cornell. Rocky wasn't so sure. He was young and uncertain of his future, and by no means had he gotten wrestling out of his system.

While he pondered his options, Rocky shared a small apartment in Manhattan's Upper West Side with Seiji Ozawa, a family acquaintance back in Japan. Ozawa, who is now a world-famous conductor, was then a promising firebrand who had already alienated himself from the Japanese musical establishment. How fitting that the "enfant terrible" of Japanese business should room with the "enfant terrible" of Japanese music. Today, Rocky and Ozawa spend time together whenever the conductor is in New York. Then, Rocky wanted nothing but out. "Truthfully, I couldn't stand his music," said Rocky. "It drove me crazy."

And so did the English language, which proved to be the major obstacle in Rocky's higher education.

Rocky had taken his required three years of English back at Keio but he was, in his own words, just a "so-so student" of the subject.

Actually, language is a stumbling block for many Japanese in this country (and vice versa) because the languages are not at all compatible. Not only has the teaching of foreign languages in Japan been traditionally bad, but Japanese is a language distinctly lacking in compatibility with most others in the world. Basically, the English language is considered Indo-European in nature. According to Reischauer, that large family includes almost all of Europe, large parts of Asia in Siberia, Iran, Afghanistan, the northern two thirds of the Indian subcontinent, and the great bulk of North and South America. Japanese, however, belongs to no large or dominant family of languages.

Even today, after twenty-five years in the United States, Rocky still does not enunciate the language well. The "r" sound gives him particular trouble. For example, "first," a word he uses often because that's what he tries to be, comes out like "fhast." But rarely if ever is his speech pattern a detriment to his business affairs; most everyone, in fact, finds it charming. He comprehends most idioms and nuances of the English language and, though he lapses quite easily into conversational Japanese if the other "pahson" wants it that way, he insists that English be spoken around his house. Certainly Rocky is not averse to using language to his advantage. Once during a trip to Japan in the early 1970s he went into a Tokyo jewelry store to buy pearl cuff links. Rocky asked the salesperson in English for the price and began to barter with her. From behind a black velvet curtain Rocky heard a voice, speaking in Japanese, telling the salesperson how low she could go. Rocky feigned ignorance, listened to the conversation in Japanese and ended up buying the cuffs at only $10 above cost.

Rocky figures he knew only about 100 to 150 of the most basic English words when he arrived in 1960. This explains why, upon his first visit to a cafeteria in New York City, he ordered the cheapest thing on the menu for his evening meal and it turned out to be butter.

"You see a lot of Japanese people fresh off the boat eating hamburgers at fast-food joints," says Rocky, "only because *hamburger* is the first word they learn."

Whatever ambitions Rocky had for Cornell were thwarted when he failed the language part of the admission test. "Learn English better," said Cornell, "and maybe we'll let you in." If there's one thing Rocky always seems to have, besides a new idea, it's the last laugh. He never did make it into Cornell, but years later he was invited to address the university's student body, an invitation he declined; by that time his blueprint for success in building the Benihana chain was already a staple of the course of study at the hotel restaurant school.

Rocky enrolled at Springfield College in Massachusetts, one of the country's finest physical education schools. He grew tired of the strictly jock curriculum, however, and accepted belatedly the wrestling scholarship to C. W. Post, where he planned to study business administration. He was still nursing his dream of becoming a 1964 Olympian, but he seemed to be drawing closer and closer to the career his father wanted him to pursue. Rocky liked C. W. Post, where he redraped himself in the mantle of *bancho* that he had worn throughout his years at Keio. One night Mandel got a call from the dean of the college. "John, I don't mind giving your wrestlers scholarships," said the dean, "but, dammit, they don't have to park in my spot." He was referring, of course, to Rocky's sparkling new Alfa Romeo.

Against that backdrop, it was not surprising that the dean had a rather low tolerance for escapades involving Rocky Aoki. One night a couple of underclassmen put a fire extinguisher in the bed of Rocky's roommate, an Iranian who was a wrestling teammate. The chemicals leaked and ruined some of his possessions, and Rocky volunteered to track down the culprits. He found them, and challenged them. "Let's go outside to the quad," said Rocky, who by this time was hankering for some action. Using a combination of judo and freestyle wrestling,

Rocky threw one underclassman to the ground. The boy suffered a broken leg. Rocky gave the other a quick right to the face. The result was a broken nose, clean and to the point. For his trouble, Rocky received from the dean his walking papers.

By this time Rocky had been in America about two years with little to show for it except checkered college transcripts. It was time to get down to work, and over the next two years Rocky proceeded to give new meaning to the word, living and breathing the American ethic to a degree that would turn a Puritan's head. Between September 1961 and May 1964 he would earn an associate degree from New York City Community College (NYCCC), stash away $10,000 from a dizzying variety of odd jobs—some of them quite odd—and wrestle his way to two national AAU titles. Spare time was hardly an issue.

Rocky's anchor during this period was Mandel, who invited Rocky to live with his family (his wife, Ann, and his son, John) in their home in Neponsit, Queens. It was an ideal situation for Rocky, not only because he had been living near the poverty level but also because Mandel was a major figure in the world of amateur wrestling. With the detective urging him on, Rocky worked out ferociously at the New York Athletic Club, a powerful training station for amateur athletes to which Mandel still belongs.

"Rocky was not a good wrestler; he was a great one," says Mandel, not given to overstatement when talking about the sport to which he's dedicated much of his life. "He was rough and scientific, and you put those two together, you've got a great one. He was never, ever afraid to try a new move. And once he tried it, he'd work for hours to get it right."

But the Mandel-Aoki bond went beyond wrestling. It was nothing so simple as Rocky's being the Athletic Son He Never Had—the junior Mandel was a fine athlete, and he and his father had, and still have, an excellent relationship—but there was no doubt an element of caretaking to it. Every stranger in a strange land can use some help, even someone as independent as Aoki, and Mandel was there for him. Though Rocky's parents were by this time quite well-off with their coffee shops back in Japan, they were severely limited by the laws of the day that prohibited currency exchange between the countries. Rocky figures that, all together, his parents were able to send him no more than $500 in the four years between his arrival in America and the beginning of his business. Most of the time the money was smuggled through in the pages of a book.

As we will see, Rocky's own industriousness accounted for most of his money, but in the spirit of all American collegians he was not averse to hitting up Mandel for a few bucks. His favorite ruse was to request $25 "to buy a raincoat." He tried it so many times it became a standing joke; to this day, Ann Mandel will ask Rocky if he's ever bought the raincoat.

But the deep feelings Mandel had for Rocky went beyond his role as semi provider. As a detective, Mandel lived a part of his life on the edge, and he sensed a similar willingness in Rocky. Mandel had a feeling for men of action, men who challenged themselves and others, and Rocky fit that bill. On the wall of the Manhattan security office Mandel owns and manages today hang dozens of newspaper clippings describing crimes that Mandel had a hand in solving. He helped catch New York City's famed "dairy bandit" as he attempted to rob his thirteenth bank on Friday the thirteenth. Within a few hours he helped track down men who held up the *Daily News* building in Brooklyn. And he was in on the apprehension of the "mad dog killers," who slaughtered six people during one weekend murder spree in the 1960s. Mandel lived on the tabloid side of life, and Rocky would become, to a certain extent, a tabloid kind of person, what with spectacular boat crashes, balloon flights, and the singular kind of magnetism created by millions of dollars. Mandel didn't know all that at the time, of course, but with a detective's sixth sense on such matters, he sniffed out a man who would make his mark, one way or the other.

It's important to note exactly what it was that Mandel saw in Rocky. The detective did not like a man who flaunted the law, and he did not like a young man who lived his life immorally. Rocky did neither. "Rocky used to bring his girlfriends into the squad house on West 47th Street," remembers Mandel, "but he never brought them home. He didn't do that kind of thing." Perhaps he didn't do it because Mandel frequently checked his elbows to see if he'd been lying with a woman, but nevertheless, he didn't do it. Neither did Rocky compromise on his wrestling training. Mandel remembers looking out his window one evening long after midnight and seeing Rocky and his son returning from an end-of-the-summer beach party. John had had too much to drink, and Rocky was carrying the 6-foot, 3-inch, 200-pound Mandel over his shoulders.

What Mandel responded to in Rocky was a sense of bravura— "He just didn't toe the line, this guy," says Mandel over and over in a conversation about Rocky—but a bravura tempered by discipline and control. You don't win three national wrestling championships by showing up once in a while, or by parking in the dean's spot *all* the time.

At NYCCC, Rocky concentrated on courses in management rather than the culinary arts. Although Rocky always liked the heat, he cared not a whit for the kitchen, and at any rate, he never displayed any propensity toward cooking. "Every morning he made me French toast," remembers Mandel. "That was the extent of his cooking ability." This remains about the extent of it today. Curiously, the restaurant concept that Rocky would create in 1964 allows a chef to demonstrate the kind of showmanship Rocky may have chosen for himself; in fact, both of Rocky's brothers, Hiro and Shiro, who are in the Japanese restaurant business today, began as Benihana chefs. But the knife and fork were not for Rocky; instead he would be the whip and chain that managed the knife and fork.

Rocky took the usual management courses at NYCCC, but he was strongest in promotion and customer relations; they would prove to be his strengths at Benihana also. But just as important to his eventual success were the series of odd jobs he took to support himself at college. He learned to read people, New Yorkers in particular, and he found that their image of aloofness and coldness was a false one, that, if given a reason, they would sit among total strangers and eat a meal. Nothing was more important to Benihana's future than Rocky's belief in that idea.

"Rocky Worked Here" signs around Manhattan could be as familiar as "Washington Slept Here" signs around Trenton, New Jersey. One of his first part-time jobs was at a parking lot on West 46th Street, where he was paid the princely sum of $1 an hour for a ten-hour day, "without the boss counting the last two hours," Rocky says. However, Rocky was to have another last laugh: Years later while driving around Manhattan, he ran into his former boss at the lot. The guy had seen Rocky's picture on the wall of a Benihana restaurant and asked, "Who's dat?" "That's the boss," he was told. "No kidding! He used to park cars for me." The man looked in at Rocky, who was then driving a Jensen Interceptor II, an expensive British car, and said, "Hey, Rocky, want a job now?"

He made $40 a week working for Horn & Hardart and, never being one to shrink from a challenge, sought out Mr. Hardart himself and told him he needed more hours. Mr. Hardart was impressed and called Rocky's manager. Rocky didn't stay long, though. At each new job he'd invariably grow restless and leave after a few months in search of more money and more responsibility.

He got more of the former in his capacity as a mover for Miyazaki, a Japanese company with a branch in New York City. The Miyazaki

movers' primary job was to drive to the pier and pick up the possessions of the Japanese executives who were arriving in America.
Normally the drivers worked in two-man crews, but Rocky insisted
on working alone, both to get the double paycheck and to use his
employment as another way to get in shape for wrestling. On other
days Rocky would slip behind the wheel of a Miyazaki limousine and
drive clients around New York for some sightseeing.

In the summer of 1963, between his first and second year at
NYCCC, Rocky secured a job driving an ice cream truck. His first
assignment was Midtown Manhattan. After hours, the drivers would
get together back at the plant and talk about their haul, and it didn't take
Rocky long to discover that Midtown was not the place to maximize his
profit. A frequent topic of conversation was the Harlem route, which
was about as popular as a tour of duty in Phnom Penh. Rocky's reason-
ing about Harlem, though, was more economic in nature. "I figured
that if nobody was selling ice cream there then they'd be a lot of thirsty
people." So off to Harlem he went. "The danger didn't concern me at all.
I was in shape from wrestling, and anyway, I'd been in fights my whole
life. Besides, I lived downtown on Suffolk Street. That was danger."

Rocky paid $24 for the rental of the truck and $24 for each round
of ice cream. The custom for most drivers was to sell out for the day
and go home, but Rocky went back and filled up, twice, three times.
He was right—there were lots of thirsty people. Harlem wanted ice
cream as much as the Japanese wanted sugar in his father's coffee-
houses, and Rocky was going to give it to them. His entrepreneurial
skills emerged, too, perhaps for the first time. He jazzed up his operation by blaring Japanese music from his truck and adorning each
cone with a small Japanese paper umbrella. He became the Japanese
emperor of ice cream in Harlem, and within four months he had
tucked away $10,000, which turned out to be the seed money for the
flowering of Benihana in America.

But it didn't come easily. On three occasions he parked his truck for a short break and locked it up, only to return and find the entire inventory stolen. One evening as he was checking the generator in the truck he felt a man grab him around the neck, another man jab a fist in his ribs, and to complete a trifecta, another poke a knife in his right leg. "Walk to the building and don't turn around," one of them said. They took everything, right down to his shoes, and told him to run as fast as he could in one direction while they took off in the other. Rocky ran about fifty yards then, "like the idiot I was," reversed his direction and ran after them. He never found them, perhaps fortunately. Nor did he bother to call the police, with whom he would have his greatest Harlem misadventure.

Late in the season when Rocky was ready to go back to NYCCC, he was approached by a policeman and asked to (1) pay him protection money; (2) move his truck from where it was illegally double-parked; or (3) show him a vendor's license he didn't have, according to whose version of the story is given—Rocky's, the policeman's, or John Mandel's. At any rate Mandel got a call that day from a fellow member of the force. "John, we've got your wrestler up here." "What'd he do?" asked Mandel. "Took the club away from an officer" was the answer.

Rocky had challenged the officer, whatever his request, then engaged him in a scuffle. Another policeman soon arrived, and Rocky used his wrestling and karate moves to fend them off, managing in the process to remove a club from one of them. By that time a crowd of several hundred had gathered on the sidewalk, most of them cheering for the underdog, Harlem being an underdog kind of place. Finally, when the cuffs came out, Rocky surrendered and let himself be cuffed behind his back. As a final gesture of superiority, however, Rocky succeeded in working the cuffs down his back, under his hips and through his legs so that they landed up in a position in front of him by the time they had driven to the mid-city station house where Mandel was waiting. "I was very flexible at that time," Rocky said. The police were not. Despite Mandel's intercession, Rocky spent the night in a holding cell. Two weeks later Harlem lost its best, not to mention its most flexible, ice cream salesman.

# CHAPTER

In 1965, one dream died and another began for Rocky Aoki. While he was still attending classes at NYCCC, he became one of America's finest wrestlers. He was the 114.5-pound AAU freestyle champion in both 1963 and 1964 and also won a national Greco-Roman title one year, one of only a handful of wrestlers ever to score such a double victory. To no one's surprise, he burned his way through the Olympic trials and earned a position on the American Olympic team. At age twenty-five, in the prime of his career, he would be making a triumphant return to Japan as a member of the American team.

But what Rocky couldn't beat was the red tape. With the United States Olympic Committee sponsoring him, Rocky had filed a petition to become a "lawful permanent resident," a classification that would have made him eligible to compete as an American Olympian. But the Labor Department and the Immigration Service denied his petition because, at the time, he was not receiving any "remuneration." Two years later, of course, after his restaurant succeeded, he was remunerating the hell out of everyone, but in 1963 and the early part of 1964 he looked like a bad risk and he couldn't get the designation. It wasn't until two years later, in fact, that his immigration lawyer, Al Geduldig, finally got Rocky his "lawful permanent resident" status.

The bureaucratic defeat stuck in Rocky's craw. Years later after he became well-known as a restaurateur and a "personality," his wrestling background sometimes sounded like so much publicity fluff, the standard-issue folderol that had little substance in fact. But that simply was not the case, and it always bugged Rocky that he had neither an Olympic medal nor the Olympic publicity to show for it. Had he been able to capitalize on them, the new and different restaurant idea he hatched with his father in 1964 might not have taken so long to get off the ground.

Rocky's decision to open a restaurant was already firmly implanted by the time he earned his associate degree at NYCCC in the spring of 1963. The idea had three wellsprings: the existing precedent for restaurant success in the Aoki family (his parents had opened five Benihana restaurants in Japan by this time, and while they were not millionaires, they were making a very comfortable living); his father's desire to open a Benihana in America; and finally, Rocky's own personality, which dictated that he, not anybody else, call the shots and put the paper umbrellas on the ice cream.

The first factor—his parents' success—might seem to have had little effect on one so single minded as Rocky, but it did. In Rocky's words, "I couldn't get the memory of that money going into the cash drawer out of my mind." Rocky had seen with his own eyes the positive consequences of putting real sugar on the table, and he remembered it. Along those same lines, it might seem equally unimportant that Rocky have the blessings of his father. Under the Japanese seniority system (about which more will be said), Rocky couldn't have gotten to first base without his father first telling him to leave the batter's box, but Rocky was almost fully Americanized by the time he arrived in

New York City in 1960. Indeed, one of the comments he made most often during his early years of success was, "My success began the moment I forgot I was Japanese." Still, the late Yunosuke Aoki had a strong personality, no matter how much Rocky maintains that he, Rocky, was a completely independent thinker. Rocky insists that it was his idea to come to America from the beginning, but even Katsu Aoki, every inch a devotee of her son, says: "My husband did want to open a Benihana in the U.S.A. My husband definitely wanted him to take over the business. He [Yunosuke] wanted him to stay in America to run the business." Whether or not Rocky admits it today, almost any young man, no matter how independent, is not totally impervious to parental pressure. Just as important, too, were Rocky's mother's wishes. They had always gotten along well—"Even though he fought with his father, he never raised his voice to me," she says—and Mrs. Aoki was 100 percent behind Rocky's building a life in America. In her words: "I was in favor of him going to America even though I missed him very much and worried about him. I knew he didn't understand much English when he went there and there would be times when he was alone, but I thought it might do him good for his future. I thought of how a lion pushes its baby lion over the cliff so that the baby would become strong and climb back up."

There was also his parents' unstated conclusion that Hiroaki would be much better off in New York City, thousands and thousands of miles away from a seniority system that would almost have certainly have strangled him. "I worried for his future because he was so wild," said Mrs. Aoki. In New York, he would be rendered less conspicuous by his environs.

The forces and precedents that would drive Rocky into his own business have already been established. He was the son of aggressive, forward-thinking parents. He had been a bancho throughout his school days. He had involved himself in athletics, long-distance running and wrestling, that were highly individualistic; once, in fact, he had declined to participate in a relay race in elementary school because he had to depend too much on his teammates. From the beginning, he was comfortable in America's biggest city and saw only the opportunities and advantages of New York, not its dangers and its difficulties. "I remember him telling me in one of his first letters how he wanted to stay right where he was," said his mother. "He said he didn't want a small country town."

Finally, and perhaps most importantly, he had spent enough time working for somebody else. Yes, the part-time jobs had enabled him to work his way through college, but he had chafed under the mandate of taking orders. The only job he had truly enjoyed, revealingly, was his ice cream route, on which he could be relatively autonomous; that autonomy alone was worth a handcuff or a switchblade along the way.

On the other hand, there were factors militating against Rocky's going into the business. Foremost among these was Rocky's relative ignorance about food. As a wrestler he had spent much of his time avoiding it (almost every wrestler engages in a constant struggle to stay within his weight division) and had neither the time, the money, nor the inclination to enjoy it during his days at NYCCC. "When I was in college, I never went to a real restaurant," says Rocky. "I mean *never*. Maybe a cafeteria or something but never a real restaurant. I didn't know much about them at all." And given Rocky's personal culinary skills, "Aoki's French Toast" would be about the only direction he could take; it's doubtful the idea would have flown. Add to this his problems with the language and his unfamiliarity with New York City's byzantine building and health codes and you have, on the one hand, a blueprint for failure.

But failure was not on Rocky's mind. Nor was it on the mind of Yunosuke Aoki. Early in 1963, a few months before Rocky's graduation from NYCCC, he had dispatched his wife to America to help his *chonan* get started in business. As is the case with many things concerning the senior Aoki (and the eldest son), the support was a two-edged sword. Yes, he wanted to see his eldest son do well in business and would help him in any way he could. But he also saw something in it for Yunosuke Aoki—an expansion of the Benihana business, a new frontier for the old showman from Tokyo. There's nothing wrong with that, of course, except that the Aokis' inability to figure out just what the American Benihanas were—an extension of Papa-san's business or a proving ground for *chonan*—would later cause a rift in their personal relationship as well as some operational problems for Benihana.

Yunosuke's support of his *chonan* was entirely in keeping with the Japanese seniority system; that's what Japanese fathers were *supposed* to do. On the other hand, in typical Aoki fashion, he did it in an unusual way. At that time, in the early 1960s, the thought of a Japanese father supporting his son in America was almost unheard of. And the thought of a man dispatching his wife, whose mission in life for the most part was to serve only him, to a strange land was even more unusual. Even today, it seems to haunt Mrs. Aoki though she, too, favored the idea. "I think I was not a good wife for my husband because I left him alone for nineteen years [she didn't return to Japan until 1982] and lived in America. But I simply could not leave my son alone. He needed me too much."

There is a popular notion that Rocky, imaginative genius that he is, sat down one day and mapped out the plan that would become Benihana, starting with the basic menu right down to the knife-wielding chefs. Not true. It happened so long ago now and in so many different stages that Rocky himself can't begin to piece it all together. The pace was feverish in those early days of the restaurant, and besides, there were two different bosses throwing two different sets of ideas out all the time—Rocky and his father. But one thing is certain: From the beginning, Rocky knew what kind of food he wanted to serve.

"While I was at NYCCC I remember reading a study by the National Restaurant Association," says Rocky. "For some reason it stuck with me. It said that Americans prefer beef, chicken, and shrimp, in that order, to all other foods."

It didn't say anything about bean curd or raw fish. (That would come later.) To one who had been in this country for only four years, as Rocky had, the study was significant, a kind of shortcut to understanding the American palate, and Rocky seized on it. To this day he gathers much of his information by seizing one single fact and riding herd on it. Then, too, though Rocky may not have been conscious of it, his parents' business had flourished because of that single "give 'em what they want no matter what the cost" principle, sugar being their Japanese version of beef, chicken, and shrimp.

The idea to give America its Big Three, in some form or another, is about all that Rocky had in his head one evening in May 1963, just after his graduation from NYCCC, when he went out for a rare restaurant meal. He picked the Bamboo House, a small Zentype restaurant on West 56th Street. The meal, as Rocky recalls, was terrible, but the conversation was most interesting. Rocky had asked to see the manager in an effort to pick his brain about the restaurant business, but the manager offered something else—the business. "He was doing terribly," said Rocky, "and he was looking for someone else to take it over and do terribly, also." He had found his man. With the same adventuresome spirit that had moved him to take the route in Harlem, Rocky signed an agreement that gave him the Bamboo House for the price of simply taking over the $300-a-month lease.

It is better to be lucky than good, but it is best of all to be both. Rocky was both, as he acknowledges himself. "I got a building in prime Midtown Manhattan territory for three hundred dollars a month with nothing up front," he says. "You can't get much luckier than that." No, he couldn't. Yet his acquisition of the Bamboo House speaks to something more than mere providence. The noted baseball executive, Branch Rickey, once said that "luck is the residue of design," and that is more to the point in this case. Rocky was going to own a restaurant in America, and that was all there was to it. If the Bamboo House offer hadn't come along, then Rocky would have simply gotten another, perhaps at the next bad restaurant where he had a meal.

And design and luck, all things considered, probably took a backseat to pure nerve. Yes, the $300-a-month price tag was good, even in 1963, but the Bamboo House was not exactly "21," and Rocky was not exactly Toots Shor. At the time he took over the lease, he was a twenty-four-year-old kid fresh out of college still trying to learn the English language. He had three principal assets—a father who was willing to help and who had significant resources back in Japan; a mother who was already in America and who would make any necessary sacrifice for the son she had bailed out of trouble so many times; and $10,000 in cash, which he had squirreled away from his odd jobs and from not buying raincoats. His associate degree in restaurant management could be considered a minor asset, one supposes, but many a bright-eyed and bushy-tailed graduate has been brought down by the burden of opening a business in the real world.

There were three other factors working in Rocky's favor, though they were far too nebulous to be called assets. The first factor was a growing Japanese population in New York City. "The Japanese people who were there needed a place to go to," says Chizuru, Rocky's first wife. "We were very limited in language, and even though we had to work with Americans, we wanted to find a place to be together." The second factor was a growing American interest in things Japanese, primarily because the Olympics would be held in Tokyo in 1964 but also because a generation had been born since Pearl Harbor and some of the resentment and anger of the war had diminished. In retrospect, the latter of these factors was probably more important than the former because Benihana—the brainchild of an Americanized Japanese rather than of a Japanized American—has always depended as much on American curiosity as it has on Asian tribal unity.

The third factor was Rocky's absolute belief in the American free enterprise system, which, as he had seen with his own eyes and felt with his own sweat, rewarded the hard-working. Luck, in Rocky's case, was the residue of design and will.

Once Rocky had the Bamboo lease, the first of what would be many eruptions with his father took place. Rocky wanted a restaurant specializing in his Big Three—beef, chicken, shrimp; Mr. Aoki, not having read the same National Restaurant Association study that Rocky adopted as sort of a personal bible, wanted something more traditional, such as sukiyaki. "Sukiyaki?" said Rocky. "Yukee!" Sukiyaki was undoubtedly the safer route—there were already a half-dozen or so shops specializing in the traditional Japanese dish by the early 1960s, and they serviced a more or less guaranteed clientele of Japanese patrons—but the idea did not appeal to the nouveau American style of Rocky Aoki.

"At this point in time I was already a far better restaurant man than my father," says Rocky. "He would never have admitted it, but I was. But after he talked to me, he found out I had learned a lot through college and my experiences in this country. So he gave in on this idea."

So Yunosuke and Hiroaki Aoki together established a restaurant that would serve steak, chicken, and shrimp. How would they serve it? Well, three factors argued for a style of cooking that brought the chef out of the kitchen and put him at a steel grill visible to all the customers: space, precedent, and hamburgers.

The Bamboo House was a tiny place, and nestled as it was in a crowded Midtown location, Rocky had literally nowhere to go, even if he had the money to expand, which he didn't. There simply wasn't *room* for a big kitchen, and a lot of space could be preserved if the cooking and dining areas were one. This was a reason, also, for the communal seating arrangement. Also, in two of their Benihana restaurants back in Japan, the Aokis used a style of cooking that was similar to what Benihana in America would become. It was called *okonomi-yaki: okonomi* means "as you like it" or "your preference," and *yaki* means "broiled," usually on a grill. In Japan, either the chefs did the cooking or a wife or a girlfriend cooked for her mate by the side of the table. So, steel-grill cooking was not an unfamiliar concept. Finally, Rocky had long been captivated by the sight of a New York short-order chef flipping hamburgers on a grill at a greasy spoon along Broadway. Perhaps it represented to him nothing more than a cheap, quick meal after wrestling practice, or maybe it was a microcosm of Yankee ingenuity at its best, but the steel grill and the chef with equipment would be a part of his restaurant.

For men like Yunosuke and Hiroaki Aoki, the next step—having the chef perform—was quite a logical one. To Mr. Aoki, a born entertainer, the performing chefs were the culinary counterpart of the old soft-shoe he used back in Japanese vaudeville. For Rocky, performing chefs were simply part of America and, in particular, part of New York City. He knew that the concept probably wouldn't work back in Tokyo, but here he was within walking distance of Broadway and there was no reason that his customers should leave it behind when they walked in his front door. So performing chefs it was. The later idea to jazz up his chefs further by giving them different colored hats had a slightly more pragmatic wellspring. "Rocky couldn't remember anybody's name," says Chizuru, "so he gave them different hats and remembered them that way."

Rocky and his father established a corporation, Benihana of Tokyo, Inc., shortly before the restaurant opened in May 1964. Stock was issued with Yunosuke retaining 95 percent and Rocky the remaining 5 percent. The percentages were less a bow to the traditional patriarchal

Japanese system than to reality. Yunosuke Aoki had the resources—if the new restaurant floundered, it would be the Aoki restaurants back in Japan that would be called in to supply capital. And it was Yunosuke, too, who had the contacts that enabled the Aokis to secure a $10,000 loan from the Bank of Tokyo in New York. Combined with the $10,000 Rocky had earned in his various part-time jobs, the Aokis had $20,000 to knock 'em dead in the new restaurant, which they decided to call, not surprisingly, Benihana. Later, in 1974, Yunosuke made a gift of his stock to Rocky (75 percent) and Katsu (25 percent), but until that point he was technically in control of the operation, *technically* being the operative word. In point of fact, Rocky was the major dynamo.

The idea to build the interior of the restaurant as a Japanese farmhouse came from both Yunosuke and Rocky. Yunosuke, descended from samurai, was still a traditional Japanese man in many ways, and he thought that American consumers would jump at the chance to see a little of his culture. Rocky agreed to a point, but was more enamored of the fact that building the restaurants with Japanese materials would still be cheaper than buying them in America, a land where a man could not save vast amounts of money by pedaling a *riyaka* 150 miles each day. So they agreed on a plan to build the entire restaurant in Japan according to the intricate *inaka* style, which uses tongues and grooves instead of nails and screws. Eventually, there would be a Benihana Construction Company in Japan that would do almost nothing besides build Benihana restaurants in America, but for the early Benihana restaurants in America, Yunosuke Aoki found most of the materials himself by scouring the countryside and buying up old properties.

It was an excellent idea, but soon the $20,000 start-up money ran out. Rocky, who was sharing a cramped studio apartment with his mother at 98 Suffolk Street in downtown Manhattan, sent his roomie out to work as a waitress at Aki, a Japanese restaurant uptown near Columbia University. He pleaded with banks to give him more money, but they saw no future for *teppan-yaki* (*teppan* referring to the steel grill on which the food was cooked and *yaki*, as mentioned, meaning "broiled") restaurants. At least two or three times construction stopped completely, only to start up again as the pennies from Mrs. Aoki's job trickled in.

It is foreign to Rocky's nature to beg for money, just as it is foreign to him to want to share the wealth, so he did not go on a frantic search for American backers. As a Japanese with limited language skills, he might have embarked on a wild goose chase anyway. Mandel was not interested. The detective saw only a hole-in-the-wall building that had had more than its share of building code violations in its previous incarnation as the Bamboo House, so Rocky didn't even ask him.

He and his father did ask Al Geduldig, his immigration lawyer. That Geduldig said no to Rocky is significant. A sharp-looking, dapper man, Geduldig was, and still is, an internationalist, a man who in his profession deals with many kinds of people and knows there's a world beyond his own borders. He loves new ideas, new infusions of thought. And he loved Rocky, from the moment he took over the young wrestler's immigration matters in the early 1960s to the present. But he said no.

"He showed me the operation on a hot spring night in 1964 right before they'd be opening," remembers Geduldig, a smile frozen on his face. It was to be a night he would never forget. "We were all standing around the table and I remember we had to take off our jackets, loosen our ties, open our shirts, the whole bit. He explained it to me very carefully. He offered me 10 percent of the operation, which would cost me about six thousand dollars. In my infinite wisdom I thought to myself, 'He won't last six months.'

"First of all, it was too hot. Secondly, I thought, if you bring a young lady to a restaurant, you wouldn't want to sit there with strangers. Third, I thought of all the odors passing through your clothing while you sat there and watched the steak being grilled in front of you. They were my reasons for not getting involved." And it turned out that every one of those reasons—the atmosphere, the communal dining, the chef nearby—was a reason that the restaurant succeeded.

There are many Al Geduldigs in the world, people who several decades ago turned away when a friend approached and said: "Listen, how about buying a couple shares in this new hamburger franchise operation that has golden arches?" When the Aokis were ready to open their second Benihana restaurant in New York in 1966, Geduldig asked him if he could get involved, maybe to the tune of $10,000. "That won't even pay for the air conditioning," Rocky told him. That was the first indication that Rocky Aoki, then only a budding tycoon, sent friendship out the back door when business rang at the front. But Rocky and Geduldig are still close friends (Geduldig still handles Benihana's immigration matters), and they laugh about Geduldig's misfortune. When Rocky opens a new restaurant he still sends Geduldig a postcard addressed to "Mr. Ten-Percenter."

Finally, about a year after construction began, in an atmosphere of skepticism and drained resources, the first Benihana restaurant in America was finished. Its full name was Benihana of Tokyo. Rocky and his father wanted the adventuresome New York diner, the kind who would respond to the exotic invitation of a place with Tokyo in its name and one who would revel in the beautiful tongue-and-groove farmhouse construction. But once inside the adventurer would find his old favorites—beef, chicken, shrimp—prepared by a showtime chef.

Well, if the world appreciated *inaka* construction or communal dining or the labor pains of one of the nation's finest amateur wrestlers, it did a good job of covering it. The restaurant opened in May 1964 to thunderous silence.

Understand that Rocky wasn't looking for much. Yes, he's got imagination and vision—he'd prove that later—but at this point he was just looking to make a living on his little four-table restaurant. He did very few advance calculations as to what kind of volume he'd need to make money, but it was obvious that with only four tables and twenty-eight seats he couldn't make a mint unless customer turnover was truly extraordinary. The only thing extraordinary in the opening months was the *lack* of customer turnover.

"Our first customer was a Japanese guy who comes in every night, every single night," remembers Rocky. "He was a wonderful old guy, the son of a guy in the Seiko Watch Company. For dinner sometimes we had the old guy and maybe one or two other people. The old guy doesn't come and maybe that night we take in zero money. Can you imagine that? Zero money? It was very depressing and sometimes we all cried about it." Imagine the scene. Rocky, his mother, the young Chizuru, now his bride, and his first chef, a fellow named Shirasaka, whom he brought over from Japan, sitting in their tiny four-table restaurant with just the silent teppanyaki grills for company. Miss the hungry years? Not Rocky Aoki.

Rocky, of course, was running full-tilt around the vicious circle of the restaurant business: to get business, he needed to advertise, but to advertise, he needed business to get the revenue to pay for the advertising. His was a "concept" restaurant, a "trend" restaurant, which in 1984 might bring *The New York Times* out for a look in the first week. But ideas were not so easily sold in 1964. Rocky called all the newspapers, all the magazines and tried to convince them to come. One day the food critic from the New York *Daily News* said he'd give it a try. Rocky rented a Cadillac, sat in the back and posed his chef as chauffeur, and drove over to pick up the critic. Apparently unimpressed by the touch of the uncommon, he wrote a lukewarm review. More to Rocky's dismay, "It was small, very small." And the world continued to walk right past Benihana.

Between the tears, Rocky and his family continued to have high hopes. When they queried the customers about the meal and the service, as they did endlessly (there being little else to do), the customers responded favorably. Lord knows they couldn't get better service anywhere because the Aokis were so happy when a customer walked in that they stumbled over themselves to provide service. The old Japanese customer is dead now, but he went to his grave a happy and sated man.

Rocky and his wife lived in a one-bedroom apartment at 310 West 56th Street, six blocks from the restaurant. Often Rocky would sleep in the Benihana bathroom so he could begin work earlier the following day or move a picture or something in the middle of the night. "I was quite worried about his health," said his mother. "I used to watch him work from morning to night and I remember thinking: 'I'd rather him be healthy than rich.'"

"Yes, I would use the word *driven* to describe him," says Bill Susha. Twenty-one years ago Susha was in the food-purchasing business for the Hilton hotel chain. He met Rocky through his wife, who managed a Russian nightclub called Two Guitars, where the Benihana people used to congregate after work. Susha is now assistant to the chairman of the board. "Rocky was considerably different in those days, kind of a skinny guy with a crewcut. He really looked the wrestler type. It was almost, well, pitiful, this overwhelming desire he had to be a success. Of course, at that time I didn't know that he was going to make it."

One evening about six months after the opening, a stern-looking lady drifted in and started asking a lot of questions. She ate a meal, then another one, then another. She went through the Big Three and all the crisply fried vegetables. Then she introduced herself as Clementine Paddleford, food critic for the *New York Herald Tribune.*

Rocky was awestruck. Clementine Paddleford was a discriminating, highly intelligent critic known as White Glove Mary for her strict tastes. Whether she honestly loved the food or fell victim to Rocky's charms and interesting story line is uncertain—it was probably a combination of the two—but she wrote a rave review a few days later.

New York started beating a path to Benihana's door. Being an athlete, Rocky knew the power of the printed word, of course, but he never knew it in its fullness until Paddleford's review started ringing the cash register. To this day, Rocky has never met anyone with a microphone or a camera or a notebook he doesn't like. Interestingly, he doesn't seem to care what he says to a reporter or what is said about him. Like the boxing promoters of old, he has as his motto: "I don't care what you write, but write something."

Just a few months after the review appeared, Rocky had to expand, knocking out space in the back for five more tables. There was a constant crush of customers, who were willing to wait without the benefit of a spacious bar; the Aokis didn't even have the $1,500 to buy a liquor license in the beginning, and when they finally did get it, there was no room to build anything but a tiny bar. But the customers kept on coming. If Clementine said it was good, it must be good. And when they got there, they found it *was* good.

A New York public relations man named Glen Simoes, who would later become a Benihana vice-president, remembers being dragged there after the Paddleford review.

"At first we had to wait outside. Then when we got in, there were like seven stools at the bar and they were filled. Then there was a bench with room for maybe four people. You hung up your own coat. You had to elbow your way to get to the dining room, literally. I remember saying to myself, 'This is crazy. This can't be worth it.' But once you got in there, sure enough, it *was* worth it."

Much of what happened at Benihana after the Paddleford review is lost. Nobody can remember anything but working. "It's just a blur," says Chizuru Aoki.

Now living in Newport Beach with her father, a housekeeper, and three children from her marriage to Rocky, Chizuru Kobiyashi had come to America in March 1964, two months before Benihana opened, to work with the Japanese delegation at the World's Fair in New York. Actually, she had come to be with Rocky, too. They had known each other since 1958, having been introduced by Yunosuke, who was an acquaintance of the Kobiyashi family. They were married in October 1964, by which time she was already pregnant with their first child. A few months later the child, a boy, died shortly after his premature birth. "I was a hostess and a coat-check girl," remembers Chizuru, "and when the waitress didn't come, I was also the waitress."

Chizuru remembers Rocky running around "like a chicken with his head cut off. He spent a lot of time going around and seeing other restaurants to see what made them so successful," she adds. "He never talked about the restaurant failing. He believed in his idea even when it looked like it would fail for sure. His energy was completely focused." Remember that luck is the residue of design and will. Rocky was so focused that he couldn't even relax at a movie. Chizuru reflects: "I remember once we went to a war movie and I'd be thinking about the picture but all Rocky would be doing was relating it, connecting it somehow to work. After it was over, he said something like, 'See, we must take a lesson from the movie. We have to know how to attack like they did in the movie. We must fight a war with other restaurants for people. We must go forward and not retreat.'"

So Rocky attacked. His customers liked the food and the service and, most of all, the showmanship of the chefs, most of whom had been trained in Yunosuke's Japan restaurants before being sent to

Benihana in New York. Most of the time the chefs earned a spontaneous round of applause from the mesmerized customers.

Equally mesmerized was the Aoki family as the money rolled in. They had never expected it and weren't prepared for it. For the first year Rocky did nothing with the money but stash it away, much as he had stashed away the proceeds from his father's coffeehouse long ago. Rocky counted the twenties, fifties, and hundreds and left his mother to figure the small stuff. And every day Katsu Aoki went to the Chase Manhattan Bank to exchange the small money for thousand-dollar bills, which Rocky could more easily put in the safe. The procedure never ceased to amuse him.

"I couldn't help thinking what the bank guys must've thought," says Rocky. "Every day this proper Japanese lady comes into the bank and exchanges all this small money for thousand-dollar bills."

# CHAPTER

In early December 1979 Rocky and Yunosuke Aoki cried together for the first and only time in their lives. Rocky was on an elevator in a Tokyo hospital with his wife, Pamela, and three-year-old son, Kyle, and his father, suffering from a liver cancer that would kill him a few weeks later. As the doors closed, Yunosuke began crying. Then Rocky started. It must have been quite a sad, strange sight: the old tap dancer, his belly swollen, his spirit broken; and the prodigal son, hobbling on crutches, gritting his teeth in pain from a powerboat accident that had nearly killed him two and a half months earlier.

"I thought about it later, what made him cry," says Rocky. "First of all, I guess he thought it was the last time I'd see him alive. Also, he saw me in so much pain and he felt for me, too." Rocky hesitates. The relationship with his late father has never been the easiest thing for him to talk about.

"I never had the chance to tell my father some of the things I wanted to, something like, well, I might've been wrong sometimes.

And my father never admitted that he had done anything wrong. But, as I think about it, maybe I never gave him the chance.

"You know, I was happy I had brought Kyle along to show him his grandson, Kyle made a big deal of him. Kyle made my father happy, so happy. He needed to feel like a grandfather."

There were times, too, when he needed to feel like a father, and Rocky wouldn't let him. And yes, there were times when Rocky needed to feel like a son, and Yunosuke wouldn't let him. In that regard, they were no different than any other father and son, but consider the unusual pressures that came to bear upon the relationship of Aoki-Aoki: a high-stakes business, a pair of highly volatile personalities, a convergence not only of different generations but also of cultures, beliefs, and ideals.

It is appropriate now, before the chronicling of Rocky's real successes, to remember the senior Aoki, without whom the first Benihana would neither have been built nor flourished. It was his arrangement of the $10,000 loan, his dispatching of his wife to help out with the business, his record of restaurant success in Tokyo that helped Rocky get started. Whatever subsequently came between them, Rocky never forgot his father for supplying that initial boost.

Everyone who knew Rocky's father remembers him with fondness. "I'd describe him as *the* super-elegant, international man," says Stan Nathanson, an employee of Benihana in the early days. "He was simply a great guy," says Ten-Percenter Geduldig. "He was very astute, very family-minded, the guy who liked to have a good time, the one who was always around to have a drink."

When Rocky and his father were feeling good together, friends say there was no more delightful pair. "Rocky is so much like my husband," says Katsu Aoki, "fond of display, fond of being a conspicuous man." What an unusual but perspicacious way to put it.

The conspicuous men used to kid Geduldig with a bit of Japanese syntax. Two words that sound almost identical to the American—*saiko* and *saite*—actually have opposite meanings in Japanese, the former meaning Number 1, the latter meaning the lowest, the worst. Sometimes they called him *saite bengoshi* (worst lawyer). "There was always a lot of giggling going on," says Geduldig, "and it was always fun to be around them."

"They were just like my son and me," says John Mandel. "We are too much alike and so were they. If I'm not here and my son is running things [Mandel's son is an executive in Mandel's security agency], he does things exactly the way I do. But if we're here together, we argue."

And usually after an argument there was a lot of what Bill Susha called "kissing and making up. That's when they were really delightful." Susha was around a lot in the early days and had a good chance to watch the complex relationship of Yunosuke and his eldest.

"You know, I wouldn't be surprised if a lot of times Papa-san needled Rocky on purpose just to see how he reacted to a certain situation, kind of like a test.

"I would call Rocky's dad, unquestionably, the catalyst for growth and expansion. He liked the night life, the restaurant world, the challenges, doing the new things. And, naturally, being a strong personality like Rocky, he considered himself the boss, just like Rocky did. He was an idea guy, just like Rocky was an idea guy."

"My father-in-law. Oh, my father-in-law was quite a man." Rocky's first wife, Chizuru, sits back on her living room couch in Newport Beach, California, and thinks back to the man she loved very much.

"My father-in-law was a very charming man. He cared for all of us—Rocky, me, our children—very much. I think one important thing to remember about my father-in-law was that he became successful at a later age so he knew what it took. He was very creative with the people he dealt with. For example, he used to give the chefs a little something extra so they would work a little harder for him. Rocky would never have done something like that."

As minor as it seems, Chizuru's point is revelatory of the individual personalities of the Aokis and the relationship between them. For as common as were certain of their personality traits, one should never forget the differences between them.

A minor one was that Yunosuke liked his drink, beer and sake primarily, and Rocky for most of his life was and still is a teetotaler. In deference to Rocky's wishes Yunosuke rarely drank in front of him, so the kind of rummy realtionship that often grows up in a restaurant atmosphere was not for the Aokis.

Then, there was the language barrier. Somewhat stubbornly, Rocky's father never bothered to learn any but the most rudimentary English, which is not really the way to do business in America. If Mr. Aoki happened to be attending a Benihana business meeting, then Rocky, or someone, had to take the time to translate for him. During one such meeting the process frustrated Rocky to the point that he smashed his elbow through a wall.

Free-floating through this charged atmosphere was the unspoken presence of the Japanese seniority system. Or more accurately, Rocky's and Yunosuke's divergent feelings about that system. Sure, Yunosuke had been more than willing to encourage Rocky's entrée into the restaurant business and to help him secure the loan he needed to get started. But when Rocky started calling the shots and making the decisions, the old man remembered with some bitterness that, over in Japan, the son would have had to accede to the wishes of the father until the time when the father decided that the son was ready to take over. He also remembered that he held controlling interest in the business. And yes, Yunosuke, the old song-and-dance man, might have been a bit jealous of someone so close to him taking the bows.

"When they had their differences of opinion over the business," said Katsu Aoki, "I tended to side with Rocky, who knows more about the business in America. So, I tried to persuade my husband to listen to him." Usually, she failed.

But not everyone saw Rocky in the right all the time. Architect Henry Look, whose contributions to the success of Benihana will be chronicled later, usually sided with the man he called Mr. Y, whose sense of tradition he respected.

"Rocky's father had a very, very high appreciation of fine art. He and I used to talk about it all the time. When he'd go back to Japan, he'd bring me back books on Japanese architecture that I couldn't get over here."

Through the eyes of an architect, the difference between Rocky and his father could be seen in their relative appreciation of traditional Japanese construction.

"The father spoke to me many times about this," Look remembers. "He'd say, 'Rocky is too modern. If he forgets this and makes everything inside too modern, in a few years there will be no more Benihanas.' Me? I tended to side with Mr. Y."

Eventually, Rocky and his father had a serious falling-out over the profits (or lack of profits) from their partnership in Yunosuke's construction company back in Japan. Rocky claimed he went back one day and discovered that there weren't any; Yunosuke said the profits had been reinvested. Regardless of who was correct—and the evidence seems to favor Rocky—it brought to a head the serious philosophical differences between them and forced Yunosuke to reject *chonan,* his oldest, and favor his youngest son, Shiro, in what became a major-league internecine business dispute.

Shiro Aoki, Rocky's youngest brother, came to America shortly after the first Benihana opened, and he went to work there as a chef. He learned the business and he was intelligent and a quick learner—much like Rocky in that respect—and he managed Benihana in Chicago for a while. Eventually, he wanted to strike out on his own.

The original idea was not for Rocky and Shiro to compete but to complement each other. The success of Benihana had spawned so many imitators so quickly that the Aoki family reasoned that it should protect its flank with its own imitation. So it established another corporation, called Gasho, and installed Shiro as president. Whatever the original plans for Gasho, Shiro had his own ideas about how to run it. As a man with no shortage of ideas himself, Rocky should have understood that independence of mind, but he felt his youngest brother—and not just Shiro but also Yasuhiro and Hiromitsu, who had come to the United States—was jealous of his success and should have put his energies to the good of Benihana. Ultimately, there was a dispute over a restaurant in Denver, Colorado—should it be a Benihana or should it be a Gasho?—and Rocky and his brother split up. Yunosuke took Shiro's part. Part of it was personal resentment of Rocky, and part of it had to do with Shiro's business approach, which he patterned according to his father's instructions: that is, buy the real estate, develop the whole property slowly, and go for a few dependable kills, rather than the quick-strike, saturation-bombing approach used by Rocky.

"In Japan we had fights but we were always close, my brothers and me," says Rocky. "Business has made us apart. Business tore my father and me apart. It is sad but that's what happened."

Today, Rocky and Shiro have patched many of their fences. The remaining brother, Hiromitsu, owns and manages two Japanese restaurants in St. Louis called Robata, and he and Rocky are not close. But Rocky and Shiro are trying. They live about sixty miles apart, and one Saturday afternoon Rocky and a companion took a drive to visit Shiro at his Gasho restaurant along Route 32 in Central Valley, New York, about forty miles south of the main Catskill resorts. Shiro, his wife, and his two teenaged children live in a modest house on the restaurant's spacious, well-manicured grounds, which include a small resort hotel, cabins, and an attractive Japanese house in which Katsu Aoki once lived. The restaurant may now be converted to a shabu-shabu style restaurant, a different type of Japanese cuisine that features thinly sliced meat dipped in boiling water.

The Gasho restaurant itself, like most of the Benihanas, is modeled after a multiple-family farmhouse in Japan. *Gasho,* which means "praying hands" in Japanese, was built from an elaborate farmhouse in a remote area north of Kyoto, Japan, that was disassembled, brought to Tokyo, and reassembled to check its soundness, then again disassembled to be shipped to America, where it was reassembled in Central Valley. For that trouble, it had better be beautiful. And it is. There are other Gasho restaurants in Westchester County and Long Island and two in Denver, which compete with a Benihana. At each location Shiro owns the surrounding real estate as well as the restaurant proper. The cuisine is almost identical to Benihana's. Shiro freely admits that since Rocky hit upon the successful formula of entrée selection and tableside preparation, he had no reason to change it.

But while their restaurants are evocative of each other, the brothers themselves are not. Shiro looks much more the conventional businessman, without the handlebar mustache, the perm, and the full-length fox coats Rocky has been known to favor. He speaks much clearer English than Rocky, but he's not as tuned into the idioms. For example, he says that he's more "stayed back" than his brother. (Most people are.) You can know these men from their hobbies: Rocky flies balloons and races boats; Shiro plays golf, the stayed-back game.

In the presence of his brother, Shiro is like most people in that he tends to dissolve while Rocky stays in clear focus. Away from his brother he comes across as an intelligent, somewhat forceful man who gets things done his way without the flash and dash. After all, he is a millionaire himself. But he acknowledges the debt to his big brother.

"Yes, I have had success, but really, you cannot compare me to my brother," says Shiro with a small smile. "In 1983 Gasho did six million dollars in business. Benihana did seventy-five million dollars. Not too much to compare.

"I carry the Aoki name with pride, and I know it was Rocky who made the name known. Whenever Gasho is written up, you will see my name mentioned as 'the brother of Rocky Aoki.' And I know a lot of people think Benihana owns Gasho. That doesn't bother me at all. He sold the Aoki name, the Benihana name, and he deserves that. If anything, it's been an advantage for me. What's the use of being ashamed of it?

"Realistically, how can I compete with him? Sometimes it's been tough. Sometimes I've felt—how would you say it?—'leftover.' My brother, Hiro, feels this way, only stronger. He resents Rocky.

"But if there's one thing you can say about Rocky it's that he has the guts, he *does* what he says he's going to do. You can pretend he hasn't and you can resent him, but it wouldn't be the truth."

As they've gotten older, Rocky and Shiro have drawn back together slowly. Now they're talking about the possibility of a merger between Benihana and Gasho with Shiro getting to keep the real estate he so believes in. It may happen and it may not. But it would never have happened six, seven years ago when the brothers didn't even speak to each other.

Rocky and his father never got the chance to put such spackling in the holes of their relationship. They did draw a bit closer in the later years, and maybe they came as close as they ever would in their unspoken communication by the elevator. At any rate, four weeks later, after Rocky had returned to America, his mother summoned him to return again to Japan because Yunosuke's final days were near. It was a doubly depressing time for the Aokis—Rocky's brother, Yasuhiro, was hospitalized at the same time for the respiratory condition that would kill him three and a half years later. Rocky generally has a hard time remembering details, but he recalls his father's final moments with unusual clarity.

"He looked terrible lying there, bloated up with poison. I remember a few minutes before he died he called to each of his children, very formally, and said good-bye. 'Hiroaki, come here, Hiroaki. Yasuhiro, come here, Yasuhiro.' My mother was standing beside him at the head of the bed. I told Shiro to give him a little massage on the legs.

"Then, the blood came out of his mouth. They put him in an oxygen tent. My mother and I were touching him and my mother said, 'Oh, doctor, he is so cold.'

"The doctor had cleaned up all the blood by that time, and my father, who was quite weak by then, says, real clearly, 'Doctor, thank you.' He was thanking him for the long care he had given him. And then he died."

The date was December 27, 1979. Yunosuke was seventy-three. Rocky recorded the details in a book he has kept since last year when he joined Reiyukai, a California-based group dedicated to preserving the memory of loved ones who have died. It is an outgrowth of a wonderful Japanese belief that a person is immortal as long as his memory is preserved by those who loved him. Such a man was Yunosuke Aoki.

"I remember when my husband called for Rocky as he was dying," says Mrs. Aoki. "He didn't want to take his hand off Rocky. I really believe he wanted to say, 'Rocky, I disputed you on many things. I want to tell you why. I did it because I loved you and wanted to protect you. Try to understand that, Rocky. Please try to understand.'"

Rocky on the *The Merv Griffin Show*.

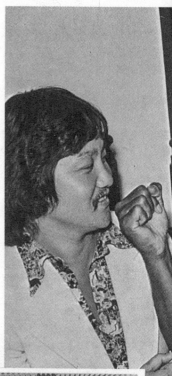

During the 1970s, Rocky and boxing great
Muhammad Ali shared the TV limelight
with Howard Cosell.

Ali, a frequent visitor to Benihana restaurants, enjoyed sparring with Rocky as much as he did the food. The two Olympians from the 1960 Games in Rome remained friends.

"Having celebrities as friends is nice," admitted Rocky, "but for a kid from Tokyo, being a celebrity is even nicer."

Rocky with auto racing greats Al Unser, *left*, and Johnny Rutherford, *center*.

His success with Benihana afforded Rocky the luxury of some expensive hobbies, like collecting exotic and vintage cars. He estimated that over the years, he owned more than fifty such automobiles, ranging from Pierce-Arrows and Cords to Ferraris and Maseratis.

One thing all the Aokis agreed on was the need for authenticity in construction and decor of the Benihana restaurants. "Each one is a little different from the others," claimed Rocky, "but they look like they are right out of Japan."

# CHAPTER

As Benihana grew and prospered, as Mama-san made more and more trips to the bank to change those tens and twenties into big bills, the need for a second Benihana became more apparent. Rocky was turning away twenty-five to fifty customers a day because there weren't enough teppanyaki tables to accommodate them all. It couldn't continue or Benihana would have succumbed to a very real malady in the business world—too much too soon. Still, Rocky and his father weren't thinking in terms of a second restaurant. "Too much pressure," said Rocky. "Too much to worry about." So for the time being, Rocky set out to make his own little four-table corner of the world as successful as possible.

Rocky got considerable assistance from a man named Al Fields, a liquor salesman, who, like most everybody, saw something special in Rocky and went out of his way to be a friend. Fields knew the ins and the outs of the restaurant business in Manhattan and helped Rocky in many areas, particularly in purchasing. Normally that part of the business causes the most problems for a novice, but by the mere fact of the limited menu he had chosen, Rocky eliminated many of his purchasing problems. The most important element in the Benihana system was the system itself—the chefs, the showmanship, the service.

The allure and mystique of Rocky's adopted country worked in his favor when it came to securing his chefs. The opportunity to perform in wide-open America at a higher salary than he was drawing in Japan could hardly fail to sound attractive to the average chef, most of whom came from Yunosuke and Katsu's Benihana French restaurant back in Tokyo.

"It was considered a reward for a chef to come over to Benihana," said Nick Kobayashi, who at that time was still in Japan watching the miracle of Benihana from the perspective of a brother-in-law. "A chef could make eight hundred to a thousand dollars a month in America, much, much more than in Japan. What a lot of people thought about doing was to come over, make a lot of money, and take it back to Japan, where it would be worth a lot more." And indeed, that happened in many cases—there are forty-nine Benihanas in existence today, and at least as many restaurants have been started by Rocky's former chefs, both in America and in Japan. But if that kind of turnover was a perversion of the traditional Japanese system, where an employee stayed with an employer virtually his or her entire working life, it didn't bother Rocky—he got highly motivated, highly talented chefs who worked their colored hats off for Benihana, even if, in most cases, it wasn't for a lifetime.

The cynical view of the Aokis' employment philosophy was that they brought over so many Japanese chefs and workers because it was cheaper. "That is absolutely untrue," says Ten-Percenter Geduldig, who had handled virtually all of Benihana's myriad immigration matters through the years. "By the time you consider the problems you had with legal matters and all, it's not that much different from hiring an American." "If anyone knew the problems we had taking care of the employees from Japan," said Katsu Aoki, "they would know it wasn't the easy way to do it. It took a long time just to settle our people down and teach them how to greet a customer in English."

Economic strategy or not, Rocky would still have hired Japanese. "Americans are simply not that adept at doing what Rocky wanted done," says Geduldig. "I'd compare it to a hockey team. If you wanted to start one in America, you'd hire Canadians."

Even if one wanted to argue the point that Americans could master the cutlery and quick-cooking skills that Benihana required, it is simply unarguable that a key ingredient to the Benihana success is intrinsic to the Japanese sensibility. Call it politeness, attentiveness, courteousness, whatever. The Japanese have it in spades, and they have never had to go to McDonald's Burger College to learn it. And that sensibility might have been as important as anything to Benihana's ultimate success.

"You'd get greeted, seated, and then the show began," said Susha. "Looking from the outside, as I was back in those days, I remember being struck by the fact that I didn't hear the complaints about service that I usually heard at restaurants. Never.

"Now, some of my Chinese friends used to make jokes about how the Japanese would bow and scrape. It seemed to them kind of a 'canned' routine, but it wasn't. It truly wasn't. I had a lot of Chinese colleagues in the business, and I used to tell them that they'd do themselves a favor by doing some of the things they were doing at Benihana very early."

Courtesies such as pinning a little flower on a lapel or slipping a customer an extra cup of sake. And remembering names. Remembering names was a bit of an obsession around Benihana in the early days. "I remember one time one of the employees forgot to use the name of a regular customer," says Chizuru. "Rocky went crazy. He was always after us to remember names."

And Rocky was not particularly concerned that he was the worst offender of his own rule. It was not his job to remember names. It was his job to be the ringleader, and it was a task he performed with zest and a certain panache that caught those accustomed to Asian reticence completely off-guard.

"He was such a public kind of personality, greeting people, talking to them, even if he had no idea who they were," says Susha. "He was really in the thick of it. The word *cute* comes to mind. A lot of people used that word when they described Rocky."

Often that was not the word chosen by his employees. "Rocky was very exacting with his employees," remembers Chizuru Aoki. "He has to be the man." "Rocky's father was good at flattering people," says her brother, Nick Kobayashi, "but Rocky didn't operate that way." Slightly more beneficent views are provided by Geduldig and Susha. Comments Geduldig: "Rocky was at the restaurant constantly, constantly. He was always looking into this or that, commenting on everything. He was very stern with his employees but they loved him. He had sort of a magnetism about him." "Even though he was tough," says Susha, "he had a way of generating an *esprit de corps.*" Rocky doesn't try to pretend that he was Mr. Congeniality with his employees in the early days. "I want to get my money out of my employees. I feel I pay them every minute, every second. If I find somebody doesn't want to work hard for me, I simply replace him. Sometimes I give them a warning, sometimes I just say good-bye." In that regard, he hasn't changed at all.

When he wasn't greeting customers or meting out responsibilities to his employees, he was eating out. Not for enjoyment, but to pick up dos and don'ts from other restaurants around Manhattan, a practice he continues today in every corner of the world. And one of the clearest points he picked up was: *Don't* keep too many customers waiting too long too often. He saw customers fuming in line, and he saw them stamp out the door. And he knew something would have to change at his own restaurant, where he was turning away business because of simple lack of space. He eventually added five more teppanyaki tables, but even that wasn't nearly enough and he was out of room. There was only one clear path: expansion. Only eighteen months after they had opened the doors of the first Benihana and begged all to enter, the Aokis would be taking their act on the road. "I had told myself I never wanted to open another restaurant," says Rocky, "but business got so big I had to do it."

Rocky found a location at 120 East 56th Street and made a down payment. The first restaurant paid for the second, and the second would pay for the third. One of the first things Rocky did was buy a Rolls-Royce to transport customers between his two restaurants. Too crowded on the West Side? Hop in the Rolls and go to the other one. And guess who would drive the tax-deductible machine when the restaurant didn't need it? A certain style was beginning to emerge.

So were certain problems. From the moment Benihana East opened on May 15, 1966, it was a smashing success. Everyone should have such problems. But it had only twelve tables, three more than the recently expanded original, and very soon it became evident that Rocky had now doubled his overcrowding problem. Admittedly, he had also more than doubled his profits, but that didn't stop him from worrying.

"Every night was a nightmare," Rocky remembers. "What am I talking about . . . every *day* was a nightmare. Sean Connery had to wait for a table. Steve Lawrence had to wait. The police lady—what's her name?—yes, Angie Dickinson, Angie Dickinson had to wait, also. I remember she came in with her husband, Burt Bacharach, and they wanted a table by themselves, without anyone else there. So they had to wait a particularly long time."

Rocky is well beyond the name-dropping stage—his problems at Benihana East were truly exacerbated by the fact that the clientele was more well-heeled and famous than the tourist-oriented group on the West Side. But if there's one thing a celebrity likes, it's a chance to be seen, and Benihana East gave them exactly that.

Similarly, the lunch trade at Benihana East was entirely different from the clientele on the West Side. It was primarily a business crowd, appreciative of the service and showmanship of the chefs but more interested in efficiency. Quite often the entire restaurant for a weekday lunch consisted of patrons from a single company. Because of its ability to service both the clock-watching business community and the wide-eyed tourist trade, Benihana was able to prosper on both the East and the West Side.

"It got so we would know the names of secretaries who would call for their bosses," remembers Nick Kobayashi, who came to work at Benihana East in 1967. "We'd say hello, the voice would say hello, and snap, it was done. You know, to this day I can still remember one regular's order—Tanqueray martini, shrimp appetizer, the steak. He'd walk in and we'd start getting it ready."

In many ways, despite the presence of celebrities and the growing celebrity of one Rocky Aoki, the first two Benihana restaurants had a lot of mom-and-pop about them. The first cost $20,000 to get going, the second only $70,000, a paltry sum for Manhattan's East Side. Corners were still being cut whenever possible—the kitchen equipment, for example, was bought at surplus from the Japanese exhibit at the World's Fair—and a whole passel of Aokis worked at the restaurants. Rocky, his mother, his wife, two of his brothers, Chizuru's cousin (who later married Shiro), Chizuru's cousin's two brothers, and on down the line it went. Benihana West and Benihana East did not, in most ways, fit the profile of big-money restaurants.

But a certain glittering economic reality was beginning to take shape in Rocky's mind—that Benihana was, in effect, a license to print money.

That reality took concrete shape when Barron Hilton, the billionaire hotel chain owner, stopped in to Benihana East for dinner one evening about a year after it opened. Celebrities were no big deal by that time—Angie and Burt had been in, and Muhammad Ali was an occasional diner, calling in advance so Aoki could buy a few bottles of grape juice, the only thing Ali was drinking in those days—and Mr. Hilton stood in line with everybody else. He liked what he saw while he waited. And after he returned a few more times he invited Yunosuke and Rocky to come to Chicago and open a third Benihana restaurant in one of his hotels, a true milestone for a relative newcomer in the restaurant business. Hilton, obviously, knew what would play on the road and what wouldn't.

The invitation was extended in 1967, just three years after the Aokis opened their first Benihana. An unseasoned restaurateur like Rocky might have been expected to bow his knee to someone like Barron Hilton. "Sure, Mr. Hilton, I'd love to have a restaurant in your hotel." But Rocky was different. If he was humble and nervous at first, he had learned to play the success game pretty early. Attorney Al Geduldig had learned that when he tried to buy into Benihana East for $10,000 and Rocky told him that that sum wouldn't even pay for the air conditioning. Rocky realized he had hit upon a brilliant concept, lucky or not, and it was his. He told Hilton he'd come to Chicago to check it out, but he made no promises.

"He wanted me to go to the top floor of his hotel and call it 'Benihana In The Sky,'" remembers Rocky. "Sure, it was beautiful and glamorous and all that. But I saw problems being up there, getting rid of garbage to name just one simple one. It just didn't feel right."

So that night, after the Aokis told Hilton they'd think about it, Rocky rented a car and drove around Chicago looking for another location. He went from corner to corner, all over the city, until he found himself near the main thoroughfare of Michigan Avenue with bustling office buildings all around him. "I was so excited that I couldn't wait for daylight to see it," says Rocky. When daylight broke, the place looked better than ever, and he signed a lease, without a lawyer or anyone else present, to open a restaurant at 166 East Superior Street.

April 6, 1968, the Chicago opening, was a significant day in the history of Benihana and the personal history of Aoki. He took an impetuous gamble by signing the lease on the spot. He was taking his act on the road, which meant that he'd have to find out about different zoning laws and the like and deal with the different eating habits of a different clientele; Midwesterners, for example, were a little more suspicious, a little less trendy than New Yorkers, and might be expected to be more reticent about sharing their teppanyaki table.

Rocky's father put his personal stamp of approval on the project. "He went outside," says Rocky, "and looked north, south, east, and west. Then he thought a minute, turned to me, and said, 'Rocky, we're going to make a fortune here.'" And they did. The same restaurant at the same location is still making about $600,000 profit per year and is one of the most successful in the chain. With no stratospheric garbage problems.

Nothing could stop Rocky now. He had been winning on pluck and luck and now he was even cashing in his hunches. California, here he came. Or as Rocky put it, "My eyes opened wide for the coast."

# CHAPTER

Looking at it logically, which was not Rocky Aoki's favorite perspective, one would have suggested that maybe, just maybe, expansion to the West Coast was not the best move. One of the most difficult things for any branch business is central administration, making sure that the right hand knows what the left is doing. But with the left hand 3,000 miles away from the right, the problem for Benihana would be increased tenfold. Add to that the fact that Benihana was still only five years old and that Rocky's central administration was somewhat thin to say the least, and a move to California seemed to be a blueprint for failure.

But naturally, Rocky went ahead. Benihana San Francisco opened on May 28, 1969.

There was, perhaps, a particular karma attached to San Francisco, the fourth in the chain. Rocky found a location at 740 Taylor Street near midtown on a rainy night in August 1968. It was midnight when he called Henry Look, the architect of Chinese extraction whom he had met a few months earlier. "Honk," said Rocky, using his inimitable pronunciation, "you must meet me right away." So, "Honk" grabbed his umbrella and came over. Neither he nor Rocky knew at the time that thirty years earlier, before World War II, 740 Taylor Street had been the Japanese consulate. It was an art school in disuse when Rocky leased it.

The construction of a Benihana in the early days was a fascinating cooperative process. For the first three restaurants, Rocky's father was largely responsible for the preliminary details. John Mandel is still intrigued by the memory of Yunosuke standing in the midst of a desolate Bamboo House back in 1963, taking measurements and making notations in a notebook. "The next thing I knew," said Mandel, "there was a restaurant up. It was unbelievable."

Not unbelievable to Mr. Aoki's carpenters back in Japan. It was just another job, even if they couldn't see the area for which they were building the restaurant. Beginning with San Francisco, which was a three-story edifice and much bigger than any of the other restaurants then in existence, the constructions got more difficult, but by then Look was on the job at the start-up end.

"What I'd do was measure out all the space," said Look, who still runs his architectural business in San Francisco though he's no longer involved in building Benihanas. "I'd design a floor plan, suggesting certain things based on the particular problems. For example, with San Francisco, there was just a lot of space to deal with. Later, Rocky bought a location that was an old Mexican restaurant [that was Encino, which opened on October 6, 1970, the eighth in the chain] and one that was a former Denny's restaurant [Beverly Hills, opened January 10, 1971].

"The main man back in Japan was Mr. Y's good friend, Ito San. They'd get my stuff and do the drawings over there. They were remarkably accurate and there weren't nearly as many difficulties as you'd expect with this system."

Then, Look would wait while the Benihana carpenters in Japan got the materials together. That process usually took about four months. When it was complete it would be shipped in three or four containers—restaurant in a box—and Look and his people would pick it up. Everything, right down to the teppanyaki tables, would be in the containers. Accompanying them were several Japanese carpenters, who were to supervise the tongue-and-groove construction.

Well, *supervise* was a tricky word in this situation. Rocky and his father were around, offering suggestions, though, as Look said, "They did a pretty good job of staying out of the way." There was Look, himself an architect, as familiar with the project as anyone. And there were the various American workmen involved, the subcontractors who by law had to take care of the electrical and plumbing work. It was a delicate balance, but somehow it worked, particularly after Rocky donated $10,000 to one of the trade unions around San Francisco to ease any existing tension.

For the most part the Americans were fascinated by the Japanese, both by their prolific work rate and their distinctive carpentry techniques. To saw a piece of wood, for example, the American carpenter pushes; the Japanese carpenter pulls. "It looked awkward," said Look, "but it got the job done." The extraordinary manual skill of the Japanese has been noted by observers throughout the world. "Examining the work of western craftsmen after one has grown used to Japanese standards," wrote the Italian Fosco Maraini, in his 1959 book, *Meeting with Japan*, "is like passing one's hand over articles of furniture chopped with an axe after caressing the work of a first-class cabinetmaker."

Benihana San Francisco was strictly traditional. Most of the edifice was made from a wood called *keyaki*, which is very fine, almost like paneling. "The closest thing we have over here to that type is teak," says Look. Keyaki was perfect for Benihana's purposes: its pliability enabled it to be bent and shaped, but its fragility was not a factor because no nails were used.

"The feeling we were trying to get was serenity," says Look, "and to do that you need *real* materials, *real* substances. Back in Japan, Rocky's father used to travel around the countryside to barter for pieces of old farmhouses, and they were the actual pieces that were used for beams in the restaurant. They'd find an old tree, and whatever shape it was, that's how it came out. The imperfection of their beams was their perfection. Any time we tried to duplicate that kind of thing it looked too straight, too perfect."

Look speaks of Japanese architecture in almost reverent tones. A graduate of the University of California, Berkeley, School of Architecture, Look calls Japanese architecture "the height of refinement of the elaborate Chinese architecture." Japanese architects did not favor the gaudy dragons and the like of their fellow Asians; they depended instead on simplicity and an effective use of contrasts. "They were like a woman who draws attention to herself by wearing a very simple dress," said Look, still a handsome and youthful-looking man at age fifty-nine, "then highlighting it with one stunning piece of jewelry." The point is revelatory. Rocky was not a man of subtle contrasts. He came to favor full-length fox coats, perms, and Fu Manchu mustaches. His father's dress, on the other hand, reflected something completely different; he dressed in careful, conservative suits, set off by matching ties, ascots, handkerchiefs, hats. "This guy looked great," says Look. Both Rocky and his father had flair, but Rocky had it ten decibels louder.

It would be wrong to write Rocky off as a purely tacky fellow who had no use for the more serene and beautiful architecture of the past. When it was possible, as in the first several restaurants, Rocky allowed the basic traditional, no-corner-cutting construction that made Benihana unique in the Japanese restaurant field. But costs and rapid expansion forced Rocky to do some compromising. Better than his father, Rocky knew the American consumer—usually discriminating about his steaks, usually undiscriminating about his environs. Rocky knew his energies were better placed in making sure the beef was tender and the chefs were showy rather than worrying about the authenticity of details that John Doe might never notice, details that fascinated Henry Look.

"Now, look at this trim here," said Look, pointing to an old photograph of Benihana San Francisco. "It looks very thin, right? Just an ordinary panel-like piece, right? But in reality it's a six-by-six post. The trim is part of the post. Now, in this country we just fasten the trim on. So our problem in Benihana was how to get this trim on without showing the nail." Look's face brightened. "Well, finally, we got around it by using contact cement."

But the triumph of Yankee ingenuity over Yankee inflation couldn't last. The San Francisco restaurant that cost $325,000 to build the traditional way in 1969 would have cost $500,000 two years later and close to $700,000 two years after that. Rocky was forced to cut some corners in construction materials and, finally, scrap the ship-from-Japan format altogether. It hurt his father and made an architect like Henry Look wince a little, but the job of dealing with spiraling costs was Rocky's problem, not theirs, and he dealt with it. He never considered himself the caretaker of Japanese architecture, and had he shown more remorse about his compromises with tradition, people like Look and his own father might have forgiven him more easily.

All the changes made in Benihana's construction were not the result of rising costs, either. Some were purely the result of the Americanization of Rocky Aoki. A trip he made to a successful Japanese restaurant in San Francisco in the early 1970s had a profound effect on his thinking. "This place did a booming business," remembers Rocky, "and I couldn't believe what they did with the rice. They just kind of glopped it on the plate with an ice cream scooper, like in a grade school cafeteria. The rice! There was no thought of presentation at all. And the customers—they were mostly Americans—didn't mind it at all." One must understand the extent of this culinary callousness to the Japanese mind (even the semi-Japanese mind of Rocky Aoki)—there is simply no more important food than rice, and to glop it on a customer's plate in a Japanese restaurant is tantamount to overcooking a prime filet mignon in Texas. It's a violation to the senses. Nevertheless, they were getting away with it because Americans, having eaten "cafeteria-style" rice their whole lives, didn't really fret over presentation.

Rocky didn't dare make such compromises with his food—presentation, after all, was too intrinsic to Benihana's success—but he did transfer the lesson he learned from the gloppy rice to his architecture. If the American consumer failed to be turned off by a major rice violation, then surely the subtleties of traditional Japanese architecture would fail to quicken his pulse very much. So Rocky implemented some American-type ideas. Into the Benihana in Encino, California, that opened on October 6, 1970, Rocky had Look install modern-looking round tables in the lounge area, a contrast to the rigid, uncomfortable furnishings in the first Benihanas, which were themselves, of course, merely a reflection of traditional Japanese preferences. Chairs were relatively unimportant to the Japanese of previous generations, who preferred to sit on the floor. "They all showed a wonderful elasticity of muscle and suppleness of joint," wrote Commodore Perry, "which could only have been acquired by a long practice." In point of fact, most experts believe the Japanese show those traits because of their aversion to living-room creature comforts. But Americans have no such aversions.

"The round tables never looked right with the traditional Japanese exterior," says Look, "but Rocky, I almost hate to say it, was right. Comfort was more important than this traditional rigidity."

Look was far less enthusiastic about another Rocky architectural "innovation"—red, white, and blue exposed ductwork in a couple of his restaurants. "Warehouse-type architecture," scoffed Look. "Excitement," said Rocky. "I was looking to do anything different." And no one could deny that in the confluence of Japanese-traditional and Yankee-Doodle-Dandy-modern, there was something different.

Even Look, however, could not help being seduced on occasion by Rocky's penchant for the new and different. Before the construction of the Benihana Palace in New York City, the seventh restaurant in the chain, Look had visited Japan and been struck by a pit-type construction in one of the nightclubs. In other words, some of the circular tables were located in dugout areas within the main floor. Look told Rocky about it, never dreaming it would be right for Benihana. "Let's do it," said Rocky, and pits were installed in the Palace. "Personally, I thought it would be too dangerous in America," said Look. "I could just see all these people after one too many tumbling into the pit." Sure enough, after a few such drunken dives by his customers, Rocky had to remove the pits.

Five years later Rocky and Look were talking about the plans for Benihana Dallas, which would open on January 15, 1976. "We're in Texas," said Rocky, "so let's think like Texas." "Right, podner," said Look, or words to that effect, so Look supervised the blasting of a huge hole that created a series of artificial lakes that surrounded an eight thousand-square-foot restaurant, then the largest in the Benihana chain and still one of the largest. "There is no restaurant in Dallas that can match the breathtaking physical beauty of Benihana," wrote one Dallas newspaper in its opening-night review, "not even The Mansion on Turtle Creek." Since The Mansion is considered by many observers to be one of the stateliest establishments in America, the compliment is a major one indeed.

But the red, white, and blue ductwork and the big bang in Dallas were still in the future when Rocky and his father opened Benihana

San Francisco in 1969. It is enlightening to look at that opening because in it were all the elements of Benihana's peripatetic early stages, all its promises and all its problems.

On the one hand, Rocky shouldn't have expanded to the West Coast so soon; on the other hand, here he was, right? On the one hand, Rocky should have had a built-in clientele with his traditional, serene restaurant in a city boasting a large Asian population; on the other hand, Rocky knew that the American customer had been just as significant to his success and he felt no special need to exploit his native connection. In fact, in a newspaper interview that appeared shortly before San Francisco opened, Rocky had somewhat alienated the Asian community.

On the one hand, Rocky had an instinctive genius for PR and invited all the right people (local celebrities, columnists, critics) to the San Francisco opening; on the other hand, he didn't have much of a central staff to help him control or at least corral the stampede of interest he had created in his restaurants.

"The opening night party was a bit of a disaster," says Nick Kobiyashi, who had come from Benihana East in New York City to be assistant manager in San Francisco. "Too many invitations, too many acceptances. We served (or were trying to) close to a thousand customers in two hours. I had so many customers screaming at me, I can still hear them in my sleep."

Too many invitations, too many acceptances. That was Benihana in 1969. That was Rocky in 1969, extending invitations to the world, unsure of how to handle it when the world decided to drop by. "There were times during this period when Rocky, without really saying it, realized the whole thing was a little overwhelming," remembers Bill Susha. "There were a lot of things he didn't really understand." And one of the major things was how to deal with the incredible amount of interest that was being shown in his product. As early as 1967 Rocky had been flooded with inquiries about Benihana franchises, not only from all over the United States, but also from places such as Switzerland and Brazil, and in 1969, shortly after opening San Francisco, he decided to go ahead with franchising.

Numbers five and six in his chain, in Las Vegas and Harrisburg, Pennsylvania, respectively, were franchises. Under the direction of a franchise director hired in 1968, Rocky sold the franchises for $15,000 plus 6 percent of the gross sales, and though that fee was relatively small, there seemed to be no limit to the money he could make in the endeavor because of the unprecedented demand. Glen Simoes, one of Benihana's four vice-presidents, in fact, originally came aboard in 1970 because he had a secret plan to work for a few years, then open a Benihana franchise in Trinidad.

The addition of Simoes and, six months later, Susha, demonstrated Rocky's realization that things had gotten too big. Simoes was to handle promotion and PR, Susha, operations and development. They both found out quickly that Benihana from the inside was not exactly a well-oiled machine. "Rocky was making money almost in spite of himself," said Simoes. "The company was rolling through as a bit of a mom-and-pop operation," said Susha.

In retrospect, Simoes probably had the easier of the two jobs.

"In public relations, you look for the things that make you unique," remembers Simoes, "and what we had was Rocky. He was dynamic; that's the only way to put it. One of my first responsibilities after I came aboard was to organize the opening night party [April 17, 1970] at the Benihana Palace in New York City. And I watched Rocky at work that night and I knew he was something special.

"I saw the celebrities gravitate toward *him,* not the other way around. I remember at a cocktail party I saw Rocky sit down with U Thant, the president of the United Nations, and talk for a half hour. Now on one hand here's a guy deeply involved with the problems of the world, and on the other hand there's Rocky, who's totally apolitical. What the hell were they talking about? Well, I don't know but they were chin-to-chin for a half hour. I knew then that Rocky could carry off almost anything."

No one believed that more than Susha, once he saw the operation firsthand.

"I was completely flabbergasted when I joined because, I swear, it was one of the greatest money-producing schemes I had ever seen. Our Chicago operation was grossing over one million dollars, big money in those days, and we were netting, before taxes, about 50 percent, which is fantastic. Labor costs then were about 10 percent, unheard of in an industry where they might run 25 to 30 percent. The figures knocked me out."

And so did the lack of a central business organization. Rocky's father, technically the boss, was spending much of his time tending to his burgeoning business in Japan, leaving the stateside administration to Katsu Aoki, general exchequer; and Rocky, general everything. "One of the things that concerned me the most," remembers Susha, "was his absolute trust in his employees. He would leave the day's receipts on the table where anyone could've just dropped by and picked them up." Actually, no one ever did. That was Benihana in 1970.

Rocky opened Benihana Honolulu on May 14, 1971, the eleventh restaurant in the chain. That meant that, just seven years after opening his first restaurant, Rocky was stretched to the maximum, from sea to sea, from East to Far West, 7,500 miles. Yet Rocky's bookkeeping had a certain "c'est la vie" aspect to it. "When I came in, Rocky had an outside firm doing most of the figures and we were always three, four weeks behind," said Susha. "It's almost axiomatic in the business that you do better with internal accounting. What we did was hire a comptroller-type individual and keep the accounting firm for tax matters."

The tighter central organization also reduced the autonomy of individual restaurant managers, who, in Rocky's seat-of-the-pants manner, had done most of the purchasing and fiscal decision making. This led to a certain chaos in the Benihana cash flow. "If there was a money problem in New York, the way it was done was to transfer funds from, say, Chicago," says Susha. "Meanwhile, the manager in San Francisco has $125,000 stuck in a bank someplace. It was no way to do business."

Along that same line, too much autonomy was doing strange things to the franchise program. The company was going to great lengths to build tradition into the franchises—Rocky still bristles when he thinks about a $50,000 construction loss on the Beverly Hills franchise in 1971 "because my father didn't want to cut one single corner, not one, even to the extent of importing real antiques"—but the franchises frequently did not share this concern.

"There are certain things that aren't franchisable," says Simoes. "In the franchises where we had management with some connection to the Japanese—maybe they were of Japanese extraction or married to a Japanese girl or had served there after the war—the franchise was successful. But many of the other franchises didn't care about the preparation, the politeness, the little things that made Benihana what it was."

Yes, Rocky gradually learned that Benihana was not McDonald's. And though there were successful franchise operations in Miami and Las Vegas, Rocky and his management team decided to scrap the franchise operation in 1972. It wasn't a total loss for Benihana. Restaurants that began as franchises still operate in Boston, Seattle, Beverly Hills, and Bala Cynwyd, Pennsylvania. The franchisee in Miami Beach built three remarkably successful restaurants, which last year he sold back to the parent corporation for a little over $7 million. And Rocky still gets occasional calls from reliable, big-monied folk who would like to buy a franchise. Last year it was singer Kenny Rogers, a regular Benihana customer in Los Angeles. "I remember it so well because he called me on a cordless phone from a fishing boat in the middle of his own lake behind his house," said Rocky. "You've got to listen to a guy like that, right?"

Rogers wanted a franchise in the Westwood section of L.A., but the deal couldn't be consummated because it was too close to the Beverly Hills franchise. Even when you're dealing with Kenny Rogers, you've got to know when to hold 'em, know when to fold 'em. "But we're still talking," says Rocky. "Any guy like Kenny wants to talk, I'll talk."

Since, ultimately, things worked out so well, Rocky can look back and laugh at the day that he granted a particularly ill-advised franchise license to a gentleman in San Juan, Puerto Rico. Soon after it opened, Rocky discovered that the man was selling corned beef sandwiches, a tip to tourists, no doubt, that Benny Hana's Delicatessen was there to provide a taste of New York City.

# CHAPTER 8

"Money," says Rocky Aoki, "is a magic thing." And in keeping with that theme, Rocky set out to make it disappear. However, he did not sit himself down one afternoon and say, "Rocky, you must go forth and spend"; it was more a gradual change in his philosophy. For the first few years after business started booming, he acted rather conservatively, refusing to pay himself a salary and living only off expenses. Like many men who make their fortune suddenly, Rocky couldn't completely forget the hungry years, and he had no desire to return to them. That philosophy was no doubt another legacy of Yunosuke Aoki, who preferred to spend his money on business expansion rather than the family. "Even after my father was successful, we lived in the same small, one-bedroom, no-dining-room, little-kitchen type of place," remembers Rocky of his teen years back in Japan. "I felt the same way, I guess, because of him."

But once Rocky realized there would be no more hungry years— barring an act of God like the American public suddenly losing its taste for hibachi-grilled steak—Rocky set out to join the big spenders.

"Work hard is important," said Rocky, "but I came to realize that work smart is more important." The problem was that Rocky didn't always spend smart. Once he decided to spread his green around, he embarked on a kind of search, his Holy Grail if you will. What could he buy that would make him happy? Whom could he meet that would keep him interested? What could he do that would be new and different? To a certain extent he's still looking for the Grail, but he's much less frenetic about it these days. During the 1970s, up until the near-fatal San Francisco powerboat accident in 1979, Rocky lived two or three lifetimes of plans and ambitions—some successful, some failed, all expensive.

Sometime during 1970 Rocky and his people made a conscious decision that he should change his image. He had already bought his first million-dollar house in the suburbs of New Jersey, but in terms of the social strata, he was invisible. "Yes, he was the little Japanese boy who became the golden boy of the restaurant business," says Simoes, "but he was nobody outside of that."

Rocky decided he would change his image by constructing a club for the "in" people of New York City. It was Club Genesis, located on East 48th Street. A fine French restaurant on one floor. A disco on another. A health club on another. A game room on another. A workout room on another. Paddle tennis on the roof. Come one, come all, as long as you've got money and a pedigree. Rocky used his own money, a little over $1 million, to open the club in 1972. Later, some money from Benihana of Tokyo, Inc., would be used to finance the operation. But when it closed down after about a year of operation, it would be Rocky who was out about $2 million.

There are lots of reasons the club failed. First, it was undoubtedly an idea that was ahead of its time. Second, Rocky never succeeded in getting the purely exclusive clientele he desired because he mistakenly procured a public liquor license instead of a club license;

thus, the "in" crowd was forced to mix with quite a few people from the "out" crowd. Third, he had originally entered the project with another private partner, but the partner ran out of money. And most of all, claims Rocky, he was stolen blind by his "exclusive" patrons. "My daddy said if you hung out with smart fellows, some of the smart would rub off," says Slick Henderson, a character in Dan Jenkins's *Baja Oklahoma*. "If you hung out with dumb fellows, some of the dumb would rub off. But if you hung out with rich fellows, you'd go busted picking up their dinner checks." To this, Rocky Aoki would say, "Right on."

"I found out that high-society people are the cheapest people in the world," says Aoki, who seems, in retrospect, to regret the Genesis experience more than any other he's had in business. "I met so many of the—how do you say it?—the cream, the 'crème de la crème,' and they all want a free dinner, a free party, a free drink. That's the main reason I lost so much money. So many people owe me so much. You name a guy and I'll tell you how much money he owes me." Two prominent names were mentioned, one a rock star, one a former Broadway hoofer. "One owes me $5,000; the other owes me $10,000," says Rocky. Perhaps his experience with this high-class brand of bolting the diner without paying the bill accounts for Aoki's almost obsessive habit of picking up checks. Indeed, there is no record of anyone having picked up a dinner check or a bar tab when Rocky is in the area.

Aside from the financial pounding he was taking at Club Genesis, Rocky also was absorbing some personal losses at the backgammon table. The games were a vicious circle for him. He lost; he paid with a good check. "I had to; I'm a businessman. If I start bouncing checks all over town, I'm ruined." He won, he took a check, and as often as not, it resembled a basketball. "I have a stack of bad checks like this," he says, holding his hands two inches apart, "I don't know why I'm saving them."

Backgammon can be an expensive recreation, which was, of course, one of its attractions to Rocky. He discovered the game when he was invited to a tournament by Prince Serge Obolensky, a Russian who is known as the father of backgammon. Obolensky was looking for a tournament sponsor, but what he got was a wild-eyed convert. Rocky was instantly captivated by the combination of skill and luck involved in winning the game; perhaps he saw it as a metaphor for his own life and the way he had built his business.

At any rate, he went after it obsessively. He hired experts to teach him the game, including Paul Magriel, who wrote *The Complete Book of Backgammon.* He converted the club's library into a bustling back-gammon parlor. And he was there almost every night, sometimes all night, always playing for money. He read books on backgammon and listened to the experts. He began entering tournaments and found that he responded to the pressure, perhaps from his wrestling experience. In 1974 he went to the world championships in Las Vegas and emerged as the champion of the intermediate class, winning $30,000 along the way. He played celebrity charity matches with people like Lucille Ball. He moved up to the expert class and beat one of the game's better-known players, Oswald Jacoby.

"I liked the challenge of it," says Rocky. "I like to make my own good luck. Anybody who says the game isn't partly luck is kidding himself, but the skilled player will usually win. Usually, not always. There was excitement, too. The thrill of losing big money or winning big money, of playing for a hundred dollars a point."

"Rocky wasn't at all a gambler when he played,' says sixty-seven-year-old Federico Vignati, an Argentine gentleman with whom Rocky often played a decade ago. "Rocky played it like a business. Seventy to 20 percent of the game is luck, but the other 20 to 30 percent is intelligence. Rocky had both. He never played for the money but for the principle of the thing. Me? I liked a little more gambling. But

Rocky would never, for example, take a double when the odds were against him."

After three years of almost constant playing, however, backgammon started to become a bit of an albatross. There were the bounced checks. There was the night at the club when Rocky stormed back from a deficit of several thousand dollars to turn around his luck, only to have his opponent sneak out an open window to financial freedom. "He had to jump across rooftops to get away," says Rocky. "Some people don't want to pay pretty bad, no?" Yes. There was the night when Rocky himself dropped $30,000, a serious loss even to a free spender. And then there were the leeches.

"Somehow I had collected around me a bunch of people who wanted to play backgammon all the time. It was bad enough that I was losing money at four in the morning, and here were these people who wanted to play in the middle of the afternoon in my office. When it started to interfere with business, I said, 'That's all.' One day I gave it up, and now, except for a few casual games, it's behind me."

So, too, is a short-term fling with recreational drugs, the almost inevitable result of meeting, greeting, and throwing around money with the Club Genesis crowd. It occurred in the early 1970s at a time, ironically, when Rocky was serving on New York City's Youth and Physical Fitness Commission.

"Once I opened Genesis, it was just hard to avoid the drugs," remembers Rocky. "The nightclub just seemed to attract these types of people. I remember one time being introduced to a New York City detective in the disco and he was smoking marijuana. Everybody did it.

"I guess I had a natural curiosity about drugs, too—why people take them, what they do to you. Remember that I had been an athlete in training and hadn't been exposed to anything like this. Cocaine, marijuana, things like this, were plants, not chemicals, too, and that influenced me. I could never have taken something chemical.

"I never had any real problems using the drugs. [Indeed, most of the time Rocky spent the whole night playing backgammon after smoking pot or snorting cocaine.] The funny thing was that I never bought drugs. *Never.* People just gave it to me. I'd be at a party and it would be, 'Rocky, how are you? Here, try this.' I remember the first time I tried cocaine. I felt good for two days. I could see the attraction of it. But, gradually, I saw it wasn't for me. It's not really a moral thing, but there are reasons. First, it goes against my athletic training. Second, it's bad for business—too much danger of it interfering. And third, it's not a good image thing. It's not a good thing for a father or a businessman to be doing."

Expensive automobiles became another obsession. He had antique cars and late-model cars. He had sports cars and racing cars. He had Bentleys, Rolls-Royces, Mercedes, Ferraris. He had a Jeep, or if he really wanted to slum it, he could drive his Volkswagen. Oddly, one thing he didn't have—never has had, in fact—was a Japanese-made car. That's probably because every other American had one.

Gradually, the cars started to resemble a small fleet, and his biggest decision of the day sometimes was what car to use. Then suddenly, he lost interest in cars. Then a couple years later, he took it one step further by losing the cars themselves. It happened when he was recovering in the hospital after the San Francisco accident. He had left his by now almost immobile fleet in the hands of a mechanic, who absconded with them to points unknown. Just recently Aoki located him and is in the process of trying to work out some form of retribution that will not involve locking the guy up. The experience would be enough to drive another man to drink, but Rocky took it all rather calmly. "Hey, they're only cars," he says. The person who first introduced Rocky to the culprit mechanic, in fact, remains a close friend.

In similar fashion, Rocky began collecting Japanese antiques. He probably has $1 million worth, some of them displayed in his restaurants in New York City and some at home. But they don't mean much to him anymore. "These are my antiques," he'll say with a casual wave of his hand.

Rocky began collecting famous friends, too, and usually they ended up costing him money one way or another. One such acquaintance was Muhammad Ali, who liked the Benihana food and also began dropping into Club Genesis for some relaxation. He and Rocky became fast friends, and Rocky started thinking that he'd like to share that friendship with his countrymen, as well as make some money on the side.

"At that time there were only three Americans the Japanese really wanted to see," said Rocky. "Richard Nixon, Elvis Presley, and Ali. I could give them one."

So Rocky became a heavyweight boxing promoter. He got Ali's people together with Mac Foster's people, struck a deal, and sold it to Japanese television. Anyone who knows anything about the shark-infested waters of big-time boxing can appreciate the negotiating skills it takes to set up a match. It was not particularly lucrative for Aoki—Ali, who won the fifteen-round bout, was promised $500,000, the challenger got $150,000, and Rocky barely broke even—but it made Rocky a mega hero in Japan. Muhammad Ali and Rocky Aoki, together, just two American boys trying to get by. Not willing to escape with his skin, Rocky later helped finance a Japanese-made documentary called *Ali The Man*. He lost about $300,000 on that deal.

But the memories of the time he spent with Ali in the early 1970s are pleasant, almost tender. "Ali is a great man," says Rocky. "A sincere man. Unfortunately, he was probably the biggest sucker in the sports business. He pays for hundreds of tickets, then gives them all away, then gives his money away, too. I used to tell him this all the time. I say, 'Ali, you need a manager to take care of your financial affairs.' He says, 'Rocky, how about you?' I say, 'Sorry, I have my own business to run. But, please, find somebody.'" Rocky's critics might suggest something about stones and glass houses in all of this, of course, but the restaurateur still has his money and the boxer, to everyone's best knowledge, does not. "It makes me sad to see him the way he is today," says Rocky.

Somewhat less tender are Rocky's memories of Broadway, to which he sang two expensive lullabies a decade ago. He got involved through Alexander Cohen, a well-connected producer and Benihana customer. One night Cohen brought with him to the restaurant one Joan Rivers, who at this time had not yet begun her unlikely ascendancy to the throne of late-night queen. "Can we talk?" Joan asked Rocky.

"I thought she was very funny," says Rocky with a smile. "Extremely funny. I liked her. It seemed like a good deal." So Rocky, who used to park cars a few blocks from The Great White Way, became one of its angels by producing a play called *Fun City* starring the incomparable Ms. Rivers. It cost about $500,000, three-fifths of it put up by Rocky.

Rocky thought *Fun City* was hilarious. Joan Rivers thought it was hilarious. They were in a distinct minority. "I slept through the thing," remembers Rocky's friend Al Fields. After the first week Joan came to Rocky and begged for another $100,000 to keep the show open one more week. "She cried on my shoulder," said Rocky. "Actually cried. I knew then that Joan Rivers was very good actress. Why wasn't the play doing better with that kind of acting? So I say, 'Omigod, she's crying. Here's the money.' A week later it was going to cost me another $100,000. That's when I said no." The show closed soon afterward.

But Rocky wanted to try again. He liked the Broadway life and played the role of producer to the hilt, driving a stretch limo to every performance and keeping a close watch on the cash register. Rocky sank $250,000 into *The Incomparable Max* starring Richard Kiley. It, too, folded quickly. The third is supposed to be the charm but Rocky didn't stick around to find out. "I don't think I'll go back to Broadway," he says now. "You don't have enough control over everything."

Then there were Rocky's dealings with the mother country. During a business trip to London about eight years ago he happened to read a newspaper story about the retirement of Red Rum, England's most famous racehorse. Rocky didn't know anything about the horse, but what he did know was that Red Rum must have been special to merit two full pages of newspaper coverage. The wheels started spinning. "Imagination," says his wife, Pamela. "That's what strikes me the most about Rocky. Imagination. He doesn't see things the way most people see them."

What Rocky saw was not the retirement of a noble animal, but a plan to keep Red Rum a national treasure and make a small fortune in the process. His plan was to purchase the horse from its owner for about $1 million, put him in a British safari park, and charge a small admission to see him. The potential seemed limitless, and Red Rum's owner seemed amenable to the idea. But the newspapers were tipped off, and Merry Olde England went bananas.

"I was front-page news in every paper in England and Ireland," recalls Rocky with some glee. "There were people carrying placards that said: 'Don't Let The Jap Buy Red Rum.' So the owner backed out. Now I hear he is doing the same thing I wanted to do and making millions. The funny thing to me is how the people in England remember this. Whenever I go over there I'm known as the Japanese guy who tried to buy Red Rum."

On another occasion Rocky's Japanese group of investors, headed by the immensely wealthy Tadashi Sasakawa, were negotiating to buy a racecourse in England for $4 million when Rocky suggested that a grand way to open it would be an outdoor concert à la Woodstock featuring the Beatles. Hey, why not? To get the Beatles, you had to talk to Yoko Ono at the very least and Rocky knew her well. Yoko had been a customer of Benihana in New York City and had often sent over for takeout food when John Lennon was recovering in the Plaza Hotel from an illness. Rocky made a deal with a Japanese television company that was willing to pay as much as $50 million for broadcast rights. Each of the Beatles could have made $10 million up front plus millions in untold ancillary avenues. They said no. "That's one thing I never understood," says Rocky. "How much money were they looking for? What's the matter with ten million dollars?"

Though he never did own his own racecourse—another possible deal for the Garden State Raceway in New Jersey fell through later—Rocky did get his thundering hooves when he bought eight racehorses. They competed at Hollywood Park in California wearing the Benihana colors, but they never achieved Rocky's stated goal of owning a Kentucky Derby winner. Eventually, he sold them.

Like the projectile in a pinball game, the ideas and deals of the 1970s bounced around and around as Rocky worked the flippers. He was the publisher (figurehead more than anything) of a soft-core porno magazine called *Genesis*, no relation to the club. He sponsored a Formula 1 racing team and even tried test driving himself at a school in San Francisco; he might have turned to driving, in fact, had the powerboats not lured him first. He hosted a weekly talk show geared to the Japanese population and appeared in three episodes of *Hawaii Five-0*, usually portraying a sinister Asian gangster. He also sponsored an Asian Festival in New York City's Central Park.

Rocky was the point man in several near-deals struck by his well-heeled Japanese group, headed by Sasakawa. Even when the deals failed to materialize, which was often, Rocky succeeded in keeping Benihana in the news. The Japanese group negotiated with owner Bob Lurie for the sale of the San Francisco Giants baseball team. It didn't pan out. And for a while it looked as if Parker Brothers would have to add a Japanese token (a red flower, perhaps?) to its Monopoly game.

In 1978 Rocky, Sasakawa, and their other backers came to Atlantic City and leased the historic Shelburne Hotel with high-rolling plans to turn it into the most lavish hotel-casino in the city. Needless to say, there would be a Benihana restaurant in the hotel, too. The Benihana sign is still on the building, but the casino was never built. There were hassles over money, hassles over management, hassles over everything. Somehow, Rocky escaped without losing a bundle but the others did lose, and the deal looks moribund. Nevertheless, it was Rocky who came away with an untold amount of free publicity. "Nothing is a total waste," he says.

They were only a portion of the schemes and dreams that occupied Rocky during the 1970s, but they don't tell the whole story of the man. Neither did the feature stories written about him, which were consistent in their themes and story line: the Horatio Alger rise, the helter-skelter buying sprees, the unhappy man on the eternal search for contentment. "I'm Unhappy, Says Tycoon with $40m., Six Homes And 4 Rolls Royces," screamed one tabloid headline in a story about Rocky, and that was not atypical. For the most part the papers were just going with the story line Rocky gave them. He told so many people so many times that he was constantly unhappy that maybe he started to believe it himself, or perhaps, he found some sort of happiness in that statement of unhappiness.

"I don't read Rocky as blue," says Glen Simoes, who knows him well. "I'm sorry, but I just don't."

"The first time I heard anything about Rocky's 'unhappiness,'" says Chizuru Aoki, "was when I was asked by a newspaper writer what I was doing to make him so unhappy."

No one knows for sure except Rocky how deeply ran his disenchantment with life during the crazy 1970s. But it seems clear that what he felt—and still does in fact—was a perennial restlessness. The man simply enjoys people too much to wear the mantle of nihilist; but most of us will never know the joy, nor the concomitant pressures, of making millions of dollars from nothing, and Rocky, like many others, didn't always deal with those pressures very well.

"When I first started making money," he says, "my personal life got poorer. I don't mean financially. I just mean poorer. I bought a nice house, yes, but that was it. I didn't put furniture in it. I myself wore my wife's shoes to save money. Can you imagine that?

"Then, suddenly, I changed my life. I started buying clothes, Rolls-Royces, Cadillacs, anything. And I kept my family poor. I didn't put the money into them. I wanted to put it where it would show."

Where it showed was in the $12,000 star sapphire ring he wore on his finger, or in the unique four-face watch he wore on his wrist, showing the time in four cities around the globe, or in the frizzy, beautiful-person perm he wore on his head. Where it showed was in Club Genesis, where thousands of dollars changed hands on one roll of the dice.

*What* it showed, seemingly, was the classic portrait of a man trying to buy happiness and finding out he couldn't do it.

Certainly all the success, all the Rocky-as-Wunderkind publicity, all the celebrities hanging around, turned Rocky's head a little. "I just thought he started believing all his press clippings," said Stan Nathanson. "I told him so, we had an altercation, and I left."

At the same time, it's just as hard for the people who are standing in the reflected light. Perceptions change, sometimes more than the subject in question. One must remember that it was difficult for the family and friends who had surrounded Rocky back at the crumbling Bamboo House to see the changes that came into his life, to see where he was going and compare it to where he had been. They remembered Rocky playing the role of eager-to-please maître d'; now he was a certified globetrotter, in demand as an entrepreneur and a "personality." They remembered Rocky's early "training program" for his chefs, which consisted mainly of teaching them how to say "medium" or "rare" to the customers; now there was an official training school for his chefs back in Tokyo. They remembered Rocky's early and futile efforts at courting an uninterested press. Now there was Craig Claiborne of *The New York Times* helping the growth of the second Benihana with a long piece about Japanese restaurants in Manhattan, which concentrated heavily on Benihana. *Popular Mechanics* did a story on the tongue-and-groove construction of the restaurants. *Better Homes and Gardens* wrote an article on the teppanyaki table. And every *Daily Bugle* within a hundred miles of New York City did a personality profile on Rocky.

They remembered Benihana's somewhat quaint credit card system, which consisted mainly of Rocky's asking, "You want credit?" and handing out a paper voucher; now there was an elaborate credit system catering only to the best customers. They remembered the sometimes painful efforts to spread the name of Benihana around New York City; now there was a sophisticated public relations wing within the organization that disseminated information about Benihana, and particularly, Benihana's founder.

But there was something about Rocky that didn't quite fit the playboy millionaire. Rocky wanted the glitz and the glamour, yet some part of him wasn't comfortable with the total package.

"I remember the first time I met him at the opening of the Benihana in Bala Cynwyd [Pennsylvania]," says Tad Suga. "You have to understand this was very exciting for me, meeting the man I had heard so much about. And he didn't disappoint. He drove up in a Rolls-Royce, wearing a silk tuxedo, red flower in the lapel, the whole bit. He did it like an actor on the stage. It was like, 'Ooh, this is the guy.'

"But yet, it didn't all fit. When I really met him and got to know him, he was a very shy guy, not at all like the image. I didn't know whether he changed in front of people or what."

Others, like Henry Look, got the same feeling. "I traveled a lot with Rocky back then, in the early seventies, and he always looked the part of the perfect flashy millionaire. But yet he'd get on a plane carrying his clothes in these two bulging, overloaded sport coat covers, the cheap plastic ones you get when you buy a coat in a store. I tell you, it looked like hell for a top executive. Finally, I just went out and bought him a real nice leather bag. With all his money I went out and bought him the bag.

"Another thing. He was taking pictures all the time, so one time I decided to look at them. Jeez, they were terrible, these cheap little black-and-white jobs. I said, 'Rocky, *nobody* takes black-and-white anymore. Why?' He looks at me, smiles and says, 'Cheaper.'"

The possibility exists, of course, that Rocky simply favored ripped clothing bags and cheap film, but the greater likelihood is that Rocky was sending a message, i.e., "I am doing this but I am not *of* this." Indeed, he had grown more and more uncomfortable in the Club Genesis milieu. He had given up drugs and had never really been much of a drinker. He had a vague distrust of many of the high-society people. If he was not experiencing the sincere existential malaise that was presented in the tabloids, it was certainly not going too far to say that something in his life was missing. He was in many ways still the disciplined wrestler, hungry for the quick fix of competition. "I needed something," said Rocky. Something to get his feet back on the ground, figuratively if not literally.

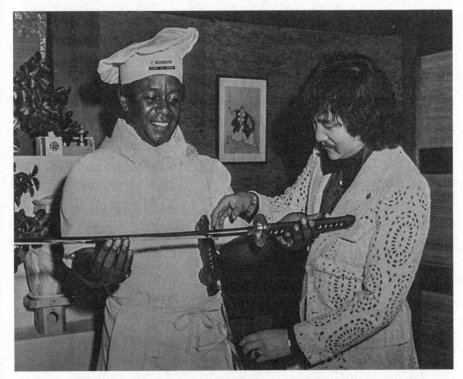

"I have thousands of acquaintances but very, very few friends," said Rocky. One of his closest buddies was comedian Flip Wilson, here dressed as a Benihana chef at the grand opening of one of Rocky's restaurants.

His long-time love affair with high-performance speedboats put Rocky in the hospital on three occasions, once almost fatally. "I know most people can't understand this, but the only time I truly relax is when I'm driving a boat at close to 100 mph over the ocean," he said.

"I don't know whether I love winning more than I hate losing or vice versa," said Rocky, "but either way, I try my hardest every time."

In typical Rocky fashion, he took to backgammon with a vengeance. "It cost me some money to learn, but I can play the hell out of this game," he boasted. After only six months of playing, he attained champion status.

One of Rocky's hobbies was ballooning, and while he was proficient in all types of lighter-than-air craft, he insisted that they were "super promotional vehicles for Benihana."

Perhaps the highlight of his life was the historical balloon flight across the Pacific Ocean in *Double Eagle V* in 1981. "I've had lots of memorable experiences," said Rocky, "but those four days above the Pacific, I'll never forget."

# CHAPTER

**W**hat came along was powerboating. It would seem, on first glance, to be a rather unlikely savior, possessing much of the same high-stakes, high-risk, high-lifestyle atmosphere of backgammon. It's a world where convicts mix with conservatives, where drug dealers cross paths with high society, where nouveau riche playboys race and party alongside old-money aristocrats. The common denominator is money. If you have it, you can get into boat racing, and nobody asks many questions. As a corollary to his definition of a boat, Howard Arneson, one of the sport's best-known engineers, describes the "test" given to all beginning powerboat drivers. "They are taken into the bathroom, where they are asked for a hundred-dollar bill," says Arneson dryly. "And the bill is then flushed down the toilet, and if the man doesn't flinch, he passes the test."

The legitimate businessmen-drivers wear their source of income on their sleeves or, more accurately, on their boats, where they advertise their commercial successes with brightly colored, beautifully painted logos. The others, the drivers who make their money in less legitimate ventures, and who keep it by outrunning Coast Guard boats while carrying a cargo of illegal drugs, might call their boat *Hellcat II* or something like that. But they were all one at the starting line.

Halfway between Horatio Alger and hellcat himself, Rocky slid seamlessly into this world. He liked the people and the people liked him. But powerboat racing provided something else, too. It was a discipline, a form of athletics, a competition. And at the point in his life when he found powerboat racing, Rocky was struggling with the realization that he had gone partially to seed. That happens to all of us, of course, but Rocky had been just a decade earlier a world-class athlete. The competitive juices had not dried up, not during all the hours he spent sitting up at a backgammon table with the new perm and the fancy clothes and the alcohol and drugs swirling around him. He was, in a small sense, out of place glad-handing at Club Genesis or rolling the dice at backgammon. He needed to get out and *do* something.

Rocky happened upon powerboating almost by accident. Some are born great, some achieve greatness, some have greatness thrust upon them, and some, like Rocky Aoki, fit into all three categories. It was in the summer of 1974 when a friend named Alen York invited Rocky to the Hennessey Grand Prix, a race off the coast of Atlantic City, New Jersey. Actually, York wanted Rocky to sponsor a race but decided to let Rocky feel the excitement of the sport before popping the question.

The first thing Rocky felt, however, was fear. York arranged for Dr. Robert Magoon, a former champion driver, to give Rocky a ride in one of the big boats (a forty-foot Scarab), and Rocky, a nonswimmer whose previous navigational experience consisted of checking the pH level in his indoor pool, was petrified. But he was also strangely exhilarated.

"I remember I was wearing a safari coat, and somewhere during the trip I lost a button," said Rocky. "I couldn't open my eyes, and all this air was flying into my mouth. It was exciting. It kind of took me back to the days when I was always looking for a challenge, something I could win at. The boat racing captivated me."

So sure enough, Rocky dove into another pool headfirst. Not only did he agree to sponsor a Benihana Grand Prix powerboat race the following year, but he also paid $80,000 for a sport class boat and enlisted the help of Barry Cohen, a top driver in that class, to teach him about the sport. Soon Rocky was racing, and the old wrestling discipline came back. He got his body into shape while he studied navigational and driving techniques. It was a sport for the mind and the body, just as wrestling had been.

Rocky began as Cohen's navigator, and he was good at it. "I think he had a sixth sense as a navigator," says Howard Quam, one of the sport's top drivers, "and that's the best sense to have." But inevitably, Rocky grew restless with the job of navigator. He wanted to hold the wheel. Rocky always wants to hold the wheel, and really, that's the only place that seems apropos for him.

He bought his first Open Class boat in 1975. The boat, named *Spirit*, was quickly rechristened *Benihana*. From the moment that logo was slapped on the side of Rocky's first boat, powerboat racing became an advertising vehicle for his restaurants, and consequently, the coffers of Benihana of Tokyo, Inc., financed most of Rocky's powerboat ventures. "I do it only for the business," Rocky once said in his early driving days. Whether or not he really believed it is moot at this point; probably even Rocky doesn't know for sure. But gradually, powerboat racing became a true passion. That it also helped business to a degree he could not accurately calibrate just made it all the more exhilarating.

Typically, Rocky made a big splash in his first-ever race as a driver in the Open Division in 1976. Running with Harold Smith as throttleman, the man who schooled him on the vagaries of handling the powerful Open boats, Rocky won the Miami to Bahama Classic, serving notice that he was not a mere dilettante looking for something to do with a free weekend, but a genuine powerboat driver. He finished second among all drivers in the point standings that year and followed that up with a fifth-place showing in 1977.

Still, he wasn't overwhelmingly successful as a driver, at least not by Aokian standards. He had an unusual amount of bad luck during races, particularly for a man who at times seems to have cornered the guardian angel market. Powerboat racing is a funny sport. A driver can come into a race with the best machinery and get beaten by a tugboat if that machinery breaks down. As often as not, Rocky's machinery broke down. Beyond that, he was constantly looking for a new way to do things, to be on the cutting edge of powerboat technology. If something new came along—a different hull, a fuel-injection system instead of a carburetor—Rocky was among the first to try it, but his equipment frequently broke down while the kinks were being worked out. "What I was interested in, always, was getting the fastest boat," says Rocky. "That's not always the same thing as winning."

But even if he wasn't winning, Rocky somehow managed to be the cynosure at the scene. He contributed his ideas about attracting maximum fan appeal; many were implemented. He sponsored first one, then two races, one on each coast. The Aoki team always had the flashiest designer uniforms—white, red, black, yellow—a new uniform for every race. All in all, he brought a certain joie de vivre to powerboating. Yes, he was a tough competitor, but he wasn't above a little clowning around, such as the occasion when he decided to run a circle around the boat driven by Jerry Jacoby during a race. "You should've seen Jerry's face," said Howard Quam, who was throttling for Rocky. "Rocky has a certain mischievousness that people respond to. But at the same time I always considered him to be among the top five or six drivers in the sport. He had guts and a sixth sense of naviga-tion. When he won, he won fairly, not by finagling with officials like some of the people in this sport. And when he lost, he never seemed to mind. He was always a good sport."

Inevitably, he became more to the sport. Much more. Had Rocky been able to script his way into powerboat immortality, he perhaps would not have written the story line that evolved on September 14, 1979, out in San Francisco Bay. "But maybe I would have, too," says Rocky, "because nobody ever forgot me." No, it was, and still is, difficult to forget the horrendous accident that left Rocky near death in about a dozen ways. And if one remembered the accident and the accounts of Rocky's severe injuries, then it followed that one would also remember his incredible recovery, and the aura of invincibility that emerged from it. "It was a high price to pay," says Rocky, "but I can't say I wouldn't pay it again."

September 14, 1979, dawned pleasantly out in the Bay Area—a lot of sun, not too much wind. If the weather held, the following day's running of the Benihana Grand Prix of Oakland, one of the premier races on the United States offshore powerboat circuit, promised to be a fast one indeed, a 194.84-mile (actually, 169.42 nautical miles) open scramble among the fastest marine machines in the world. The race would be unusual in that the course would pass the start-finish line (near the St. Francis Yacht Club in San Francisco) eight times, affording the spectators more then the usual number of opportunities to ooh and ahh at the speeding boats while shielding their ears from the thundering noise.

By 1979 Rocky had been in the sport for five years. He was not only one of the sport's top drivers but also in all probability its number one benefactor, sponsoring not one, but two big races. The other one had been held in July—his Benihana Grand Prix at Point Pleasant Beach in New Jersey. Aoki and several other drivers were still in contention for the national driving title, and a victory in Oakland would nearly clinch it, as well as supply some momentum for the world championships in Milan, Italy, two months later. Aoki wanted the Grand Prix badly. He had won big circuit races before, but he had never been a national champion. And he wasn't accustomed to not being champion.

Aoki wanted it so badly, in fact, that he had two boats ready for the occasion. One was his own yellow *Benihana,* one of only a handful of new tunnel-hull, catamaran-type boats on the circuit. The "cat" was built for speed, its design creating a lift similar to that of an airplane wing, minimizing drag and allowing a faster run over calmer water. However, to guard against the sometimes rough Bay Area weather, Aoki had hedged his bet by having available a thirty-eight-foot boat of the traditional deep-vee construction, whose strakes and chines allowed it to cut through rough water at maximum speed. Having only a single plane, the deep-vee offered less stress and was considered safer in rougher weather.

The deep-vee boat didn't belong to Aoki. He had recently sold his own deep-vee to a buyer in Detroit and didn't have another on hand, so he was negotiating a possible deal with a boat owner in Detroit named Jerry Dehenau. The boat, a thirty-eight-foot Cobra named *Mollewood,* had been built by a marine company owned by a well-known circuit driver named Joel Halpern, who would be killed in a starting line accident a few years later. Aoki probably would have had to pay $10,000 to $20,000 to lease the boat, the price tag depending on whether or not he used the boat in the race.

Around noon on the fourteenth, Rocky decided *Mollewood* needed a test before he could consummate the deal. First he talked some business over the phone with Al Geduldig. As usual, Geduldig asked why he was risking his life going 110 mph in a boat. And as usual Rocky laughed him off. Rocky and his throttleman-mechanic, Errol Lanier, met with Dehenau at a yacht club on the Oakland side of San Francisco Bay to take the boat out beyond the Golden Gate Bridge into the Pacific Ocean, where the race would be contested. Almost every one of the giant, powerful machines in the Open Division, the circuit's most prestigious classification, required a driver, who held the wheel, and a throttleman, who controlled the speed, usually in consultation with the driver. On this day, Lanier, who worked as a fireman in Fort Lauderdale, Florida, would control more than Rocky Aoki's speed; he would control his destiny.

It was to be a short run. Aoki didn't even wear one of the eye-catching racing uniforms—he called them "sexy"—he'd have on the next day; blue jeans, a T-shirt, and a life jacket (he was not the best of swimmers) would be enough. He thought about removing the expanse of gold jewelry that tattooed the upper part of his body, not to mention the Rolex watch valued at $36,000, "but I thought I'd only be out for ten minutes, not three days." There wasn't another driver in sight as Dehenau, Lanier, and Aoki climbed in *Mollewood* and roared away from the pier.

Even with the nice weather and a calm ocean, the stretch of ocean around the Golden Gate had to be reckoned with. Three years earlier in another race in those waters Aoki had spun twice under the bridge. "I had a scary feeling," he said after that race, in which he finished second. "I know it's a rough race. I don't like water at all. In this rough water if you push hard, you break down." Arneson called the stretch by the bridge "the most treacherous water around," and he, as president of the Pacific Offshore Powerboat Association, was as familiar with the area waters as anyone. Another driver, Tony Garcia, the 1983 world champion, called it the "potato patch."

Rocky started off, and Lanier throttled the boat up to 50, 60, then 70 mph. It was running smoothly. If the weather was rough the next day, this would be the boat. Aoki wasn't crazy about that possibility because Dehenau didn't want him to repaint it with the Benihana logo just for one race, but it was the only way to go if conditions dictated.

Lanier pushed *Mollewood* to 80 mph. Rocky remembers feeling calm as he gazed over the vast expanse of the Golden Gate Bridge about a mile away. But as they got nearer the bridge, maybe five minutes into the test run, something didn't feel right to Lanier and he cut back to about 70 mph. Rocky may or may not have been aware of it because the bits and pieces of the brief test run, and in fact, his every activity of the previous few days, became a little jumbled after what happened next.

Suddenly, the boat just shattered, disintegrated. To this day no one is quite sure why, but Lanier doesn't remember any big wave "before the lights went out." Rocky doesn't remember anything, and with good reason. "Rocky Aoki's speedboat disintegrated near the Golden Gate Bridge," wrote the late *New York Times* columnist Red Smith, "and so did Rocky." It was about as accurate a description as any. So was this, from *Sports Illustrated's* Doug Looney, profiling Rocky in the magazine *Success*: "His body was ripped, torn, punctured, dislocated, twisted, folded, spindled and mutilated." And that wasn't an overstatement. He was kept alive only by the presence of two big L's—Luck and Lanier.

Lanier was knocked unconscious only for a few moments. When he came to, he found himself thrashing around in the water in a mild state of shock. When his senses returned, the first thing he thought of was Rocky because he knew he was a poor swimmer. He spotted him nearby, swam over and found Rocky on his back, eyes rolled back in his head, not breathing. All in all, Rocky presented a rather poor survival profile even to a fireman accustomed to dealing with life and death.

Lanier tried to climb onto what was left of the boat to do his work while keeping Rocky's body in the water; he was fortunate that Rocky's life jacket and crash helmet kept him afloat and in position. He began administering mouth-to-mouth resuscitation and splashing water in Rocky's face to get him to respond. "Chief, stay with me!"

Lanier hollered. "Stay with me!" Meanwhile, he began searching for Dehenau out of the corner of his eye. The only good news was that he was conscious. But the boat owner was in severe pain and bleeding heavily from a severed main artery in his arm. And sharks were about. And Dehenau was drifting out to sea.

Finally, Rocky started breathing on his own, haltingly, and Lanier tried to secure him to the boat's flag post with a piece of the rubber rubbing-strake that had torn off at impact so he could swim after Dehenau, who could have bled to death. But he couldn't quite manage it and stayed with Rocky. Providentially, a small boat was on its way to assist Dehenau, and a couple of fishing boats had spotted Rocky and Lanier. The average man would have hoisted Rocky into one of those fishing boats, but Lanier's experience told him that could be fatal if Rocky had extensive internal injuries, which turned out to be the case. So he waited, and a few minutes later a small whaler, which had lower sides, came by, and Lanier and the three people aboard hoisted Rocky up. Lanier instructed the men to keep talking to Rocky, to try and keep him conscious. Then he swam over to join Dehenau, who had by that time been picked up by a Coast Guard cutter. Lanier ordered pressure to be put on Dehenau's open wound. In retrospect, it probably saved his life, though the boat owner did suffer some permanent nerve damage to his arm.

The men in the whaler took Rocky to a Coast Guard station on a far shore, rather than to the near shore. No one found out if they were aware that there was a station on that shore, but it was another stroke of luck because the Coast Guard knew where to take him—to the Letterman Army Hospital on the shore of the bay in the Presidio area of San Francisco. "I shudder to think what would've happened if Rocky had landed up in some nice hospital instead of a trauma center," said Glen Simoes, who was at the race. "They would've prayed for him and treated him nice, but they wouldn't have saved his life.

"At Letterman, the medical staff was used to seeing wounded soldiers and suicide cases, successful and unsuccessful, from the Golden Gate Bridge. And some of the successes looked better than Rocky Aoki."

When Aoki arrived at the hospital, the doctors determined that he had little or no pulse, so they ripped him open and began open-heart massage. It was a clean cut, but Rocky still wears the zipper-scar down the middle of his chest. Then they closed him up and went to work on the remainder of his extensive injuries. One problem was his liver, which had been sliced open as cleanly as a Benihana chef fillets a piece of beef at the hibachi. It was oozing blood, and the doctors had to remove his spleen and gall bladder to get at the liver. Then they realized that his aorta was split and bleeding, and to let that continue would be to watch him choke on his own blood. So they needed to do a bypass. But his blood had to be thinned on a bypass machine to perform that operation, and that was entirely too risky. So they had to wait until the next day to do a bypass.

"I don't give you forty cents for his chances," a surgeon told Simoes. "Frankly, I think he's a dead man."

Simoes began the grim task of calling Rocky's friends, family, and business associates to tell them that the boss might not make it. His mother and a Japanese business associate, Tadashi Sasakawa, flew in from Japan. His brother Shiro flew in from New Jersey. His wife and Simoes stayed at his bedside. The other drivers streamed in continuously. The Bay Area newspapers ran daily updates on his condition. If only he had been awake to calculate the large amount of free publicity he was getting for Benihana . . .

Finally, after three days of unconsciousness, he woke up. He remembers trying to mumble, "What is this?" and discovering he had a mouthful of tubes. He remembers everybody cheering when he opened his eyes. He's not quite sure why he regained consciousness at that moment, but the first thing he felt was pain. The intense pain had finally cut through the extensive shock that his system had undergone.

It was everywhere—in his legs, his arms, his chest, and his hips. He remembers looking at his chest and seeing the stainless steel pins and trying to figure out why he looked like a human sleeping bag, but he just couldn't remember anything. Sasakawa came over and gently shook his hand, which brought him only more pain. The doctors, perhaps understandably, had missed an injury—he had a couple of broken bones in his hand.

One of the first things he said, in a very hoarse voice to Simoes, was "water, water." Then "newspaper, newspaper." Simoes figured Rocky wanted to know (1) how he got there, and (2) how extensively the story had been covered. And not necessarily in that order. His biggest fear was that the massive internal injuries would slowly kill him and nobody would tell him. "You know how they tell a cancer patient everything's fine and a little while later the guy's dead?" said Rocky. "That's how I felt."

But soon, the indomitable Aoki will took over. Like many successful people who had worked their way to the top, he believed most of all in himself, in the singularity of his chosen mission. He decided to interpret his miraculous escape from death as a sign of his invincibility, rather than as a warning to slow down. This wasn't a religious or particularly mystical decision, but just another conscious realization that, for the most part, he could—and *should*—continue to do what he wanted to do. He began to think about his own Benihana catamaran and his chances of winning a world championship and the publicity and big bucks that could bring to his restaurants, and anyway, he could cut a little hole in the cast on his hand, which would enable him to grip the steering wheel and . . .

So after two weeks in the hospital, he asked Simoes to ship his boat to Milan for the world championships in a few weeks. There was a unanimous consensus of opinion about Rocky when his family and friends heard that order: "He's crazy."

# CHAPTER

The severity of his injuries eventually got through to Rocky. No, he could not race in the world championships weeks later. He'd be lucky if he ever got in a powerboat again, or more realistically, he'd be lucky if the delicate bionics that represented his body kept working. He had—still has, as a matter of fact—an aorta made of Dacron (if it breaks some day, he has about four minutes to get to a hospital), a steel rod in his leg, and a zipper down his chest.

Even Rocky was glum during his recovery. "Honestly, I think that's the only time I've ever seen him blue," says Simoes, who has been with him since 1970. "But anybody would've been blue after going through what he went through. It's just much harder for a person like Rocky to be captive to his bed." For almost six months he stayed at his New Jersey home, shuttling his Miami-based employees up once a week for conferences and basically running the company by phone. The rest of the time he thought about his life.

"The accident changed me greatly," says Rocky. "The way I looked at it, God had given me another chance to live, and nobody was going to tell me how to live it." (As if someone had been telling him how to live it before.) Simoes expresses the same feeling in different terms. "Rocky's always had a sense of invincibility about himself. When he survived that accident, I said to myself, 'All it's done is to strengthen that sense of invincibility.' Sure enough, he said to me later, 'If I was meant to go, I would've gone then.'"

Having begun the second of his nine lives, Rocky set out to take even more control of his destiny than he had previously. One of the biggest business decisions of his career, in fact, was made during his recovery. Three years earlier Rocky had signed a twenty-five-year contract with Hardwicke Companies, Inc., a Miami-based management firm. It came about basically because of Rocky's personal friendship with Hardwicke's president, and from the beginning, it had never provided Rocky with either the expected increase in profits for Benihana or the personal freedom from running the business that Rocky had hoped for. "I admit that I made a mistake, and it was probably my biggest loss in business. [It cost Benihana about $5 million to get out of the Hardwicke deal.] I am still, in a sense, feeling that association. Because Hardwicke is based in Miami, I moved my main offices down there. Now once, sometimes twice, a week I have to fly between Miami and New Jersey."

Second, Rocky decided during his recuperation to end his fifteen-year marriage to Chizuru, from whom he was already separated. "Chizuru and I had discussed divorce for some time," said Rocky. "Now with the accident, it was just a general feeling I had, to try and start things over. [In 1981, he would marry Pamela Hilburger.] Like everybody else, I had in the back of my mind that I would die some time, but now I became convinced that it would be by old age, not by an accident."

The conventional medical wisdom said that, as long as Rocky was careful, he could lead an almost normal life, the zipper scar and the Dacron aorta and the multiscarred legs notwithstanding. "You know what they could do with conventional medical wisdom," said Rocky. So Rocky took his broken body and his unbroken will to a place out of the medical mainstream—the Sports Training Institute (STI) in New York City.

At the time that Rocky approached STI, its founder and manager, Michael O'Shea, was operating an intensive, Nautilus machine-oriented workout and injury rehabilitation program for professional athletes. His clients at the time included members of the New York Knicks basketball team and tennis stars like Chris Evert and Billie Jean King. Rocky really didn't qualify. He wasn't a high-caliber professional athlete, and besides, the rehabilitation he needed was more substantial than STI was accustomed to.

Naturally, O'Shea took him in.

"Well, how can you turn Rocky down?" says O'Shea, a lean, tightly muscled string bean of a man who still calls all the shots at his gym, which today attracts big names (Jane Fonda, Jeremy Irons) and no-names in equal numbers. "Hell, Rocky was not only accepted, he was almost my partner by the time he got done talking. You really have to be careful. You don't want to get swallowed up in Rocky.

"But you know, the way he runs his business is entirely different from the way he trained when he came in here. He was a lot of hype, a lot of glitz with his business. But when he trained, no one—and I mean no one—worked harder. When it comes to exercising and recovering from the injuries Rocky had, all the talk and promotion in the world isn't going to get it done. And Rocky got it done." O'Shea begins rifling through the drawers in his office, trying to find Rocky's post-crash X-rays. "They are positively amazing. Our physical therapy department still uses them as a case history of how far you can come back." Rocky's business is a blueprint for success at the Harvard Business School, his bones a blueprint for success at the Sports Training Institute. Not a bad double.

O'Shea continues: "Rocky had a lot of specific problems, but one of the biggest was 'dropped foot.' He could push his foot down but he couldn't bring it back up because of damage to both the nerves and the muscles.

"He didn't see a lot of progress for the first few months, and he was right. There wasn't a lot you could do with Rocky because he was simply too banged up, and what you could do was extremely painful for him. And as bad as that was, it was worse mentally, knowing how far he had to go.

"But Rocky had been a wrestler, and wrestlers are, well, just a little different. You combine that with his being Japanese, and you have the profile of a very, very hard trainer. I see a lot of athletes who just aren't willing to pay the price, guys who can't come back from knee surgery or a torn Achilles tendon. But Rocky had so much more, and he just grinned and bore it."

His colleagues on the powerboat circuit, perhaps for the first time, got a glimpse of a different Rocky, a man who has more than a bright yellow suit and a wad of money.

"I really believe Rocky gained tremendously in respect among the drivers and other people in the sport during this time," says Gloria Crimmins, a well-known powerboat publicist and long-time follower of the sport. "When he first came into racing, his philosophy was like most of the others who come in—that you can buy everything. His thinking was, 'Let's buy, buy, buy, buy, so we can win, win, win, win.' But after the accident, we saw something else. We saw the courage, the real interest he had in the sport, the indomitable spirit kind of thing. You could see the change in the way other people looked at him. He had a new kind of respect, and he deserved it."

By 1981, two years after the accident, Rocky had targeted his return date—Wednesday, July 14, 1982, the Benihana Grand Prix Offshore Powerboat Race off Point Pleasant Beach in New Jersey.

Rocky's own race. Rocky's own people. Just a few miles south of the giant media center of New York City. Well, you wouldn't think he'd creep back silently in the night.

"Yes, I probably could've come back sooner," Rocky admitted, "but I didn't want to waste the publicity."

Or he could have not come back at all. "Would I have come back?" asks John Bochis, a fellow driver, rhetorically. "No way." You have to understand that Bochis goes around with a pack of cigarettes rolled up in his T-shirt and is nicknamed "Crazy Greek." Lots of crazy Greeks wouldn't have come back. Lots of crazy Japanese wouldn't have come back. Most everybody wouldn't have come back.

"To me, it wasn't a matter of *if*," says Rocky, "but a matter of *when*."

About three weeks before the Benihana race that Rocky had selected for his return, he, comedian Flip Wilson, and Howard Quam went for a test run on Lake Erie. Wilson was a trusted friend with whom Rocky wanted to share the experience. Quam was a colleague who owed Rocky a favor. Back in 1979, when Rocky finally realized he was too broken-up to race in the world championships, he paid for *Benihana* to be shipped to Italy so that Quam could drive it. He finished fifth. "Anytime you need a favor," Quam told him, "let me know." The time was now. When Rocky indicated he'd be making a comeback, Quam offered his new boat, a 37½-foot Active catamaran named *Flap Jack* (Quam owns a stack of pancake houses around Chicago) to Rocky. Rocky would drive, Quam would throttle, and the boat would be renamed, of course, *Benihana*.

"I fell in love again during that test," says Rocky. "The test was great. I remember how excited I was before we started out. Not nervous, excited. And everything went smoothly. I knew we were ready."

So ready, in fact, that Rocky exuded nothing but confidence before the race. He never withered under the constant glare of the cameras; indeed, he seemed almost to "expand," as one observer put it. At the drivers' meeting the morning of the race, there was some question about the course. "Don't worry," Rocky said to the other drivers with a smile. "Just follow me." Still, there was one hedge. Rocky insisted on taking along a navigator, Mike Nebus, mainly in the event that his knee popped out and he'd need a replacement driver. Even at that he made a joke. "If I cannot do it," he said, "I simply throw myself in the water at some checkpoint." A checkpoint near the spectator-filled shoreline, no doubt.

Rocky was so single-minded in his goal that he professed to being unconcerned by a disturbing phone call he received at about two o'clock the morning of the race. It was an astrologer, a friend of a friend, bearing bad news. "The stars bode bad for you, Rocky," she said. The message was that another crippling injury or even death could be waiting if he got behind the wheel. Astrology still tags along with Rocky. His wife, Pamela, is a fairly avid peruser of the charts, and she frequently jots down the notation AVAT (Avoid Air Travel) beside certain astrologically ominous dates in his calendar. Rocky neither discounts his wife's worries nor governs his travel by them. "I don't count astrology out," he says, "but I don't count it in, either." To the astrologer who called him before the Point Pleasant race, he offered the gentle Japanese counterpart of "pfshaw." Then he went back to sleep.

Attesting to the fact that Rocky's foremost goal is to win and not just to do things the spectacular way—remember his conservative backgammon style—he and Quam mapped out a cautious strategy for the race, one that would add a mile to their course but would make it easier to hit a certain troublesome buoy seven miles offshore. It worked. Several drivers had trouble at that buoy. Others, including defending world champion Jacoby, had engine trouble. Rocky, Quam, and Nebus had only a little trouble. Twice during the race Rocky inadvertently tripped his kill switch—the cord running from each crewman's life jacket to the ignition that automatically cuts the engine if he's thrown from the cockpit—and he and Quam exchanged a few nasty words; indeed, one of the reasons for their enduring relationship is their ability to jaw at each other and forget it immediately. But basically, *Benihana* was in control from start to finish. It tripped along the tranquil Atlantic at an average of 80.25 mph for the 208-mile race (then a record), and Rocky did some more legend making.

"It was just an unbelievable feeling when I came across the finish line," said Rocky. "There were maybe 250,000 people in Point Pleasant to see the race. It seemed like all of them were on shore shouting, cheering. '*Rah*-kee! *Rah*-kee!' I don't think I'll ever forget it."

"What it was," says Gloria Crimmins, "was a damn B movie. Nobody could've scripted it better."

Or scripted the sequel worse. The scene was the first Kiekhaefer-St. Augustine Classic race in the waters off St. Augustine, Florida. On September 11, 1982, a scant two months after the *Rah*-kee! *Rah*-kee! cheers had been heard along the Jersey shore, Aoki, Quam, and Nebus were ready to do it again. But Fate once again reached in and deposited Rocky Aoki in the arms of Neptune. The accident happened early in the race. Rocky in *Benihana,* Tony Garcia in *Arneson,* and Eddie Trotta in *Rampage* were running neck-and-neck as they passed the first checkpoint the second time around. Suddenly, Rocky's boat headed skyward, "taking a header," as Garcia explained later, "that just wouldn't quit." Actually, Rocky had had a split-second foreshadowing of danger when the boat started vibrating. "Omigod," Rocky thought, "something's going to happen."

Rocky remembers two questions racing through his brain when he was up in the air with the boat: "Should I stay with the boat or bail out?" He decided to stay with the boat, and there he was, still in the driver's seat, when the boat came down on that side, its weakest part. And there he went as the rushing ocean propelled Rocky out like a water cannon.

"I felt the water come in right away," said Rocky. "I remember feeling the pressure in my ears and eyes. Then I conked out."

Rocky landed up about seventy-five feet from the boat. Quam and Nebus had stayed with the boat because their section hadn't broken; in fact, when Garcia looked back, he thought everything was okay because the boat had righted itself when they landed. But those drivers and spectators who had watched Rocky cannonball through the air didn't think he was all right. When Rocky regained consciousness a few minutes later, he wasn't so sure.

"My first thought was that maybe I had to help the other guys," remembers Rocky. "But then I felt so much pain I could only think of that. I tried moving my arms and they were okay. My neck pained but I could move it. Then I tried my hip and it was locked, locked solid. My thought then was that I broke my back. Then I tried my legs and they were locked, too. Then I saw my uniform, which was half gone. I was almost naked and I figured I had a big wound somewhere. I figured I'd lie there bleeding to death."

Quam, meanwhile, had been only slightly shaken up and was able to swim over and check on Rocky's condition.

"I can still see him floating there, arms folded, legs straight out," says Quam. "I remember him saying, 'My legs hurt but other than that I'm fine.' Now here's a guy who had just flown out of a boat on a tunnel of water—I mean, it was the most unbelievable thing I've ever seen—and he was so composed, so calm." As he was being lifted onto the rescue boat that arrived a few minutes later, Rocky did whisper his one fear to Quam: "I wonder if there are any sharks."

On the trip to Flagler Hospital in St. Augustine, Rocky was thinking only of what he would tell Pamela. He instructed Glen Simoes to tell her that he had hurt his finger. Wonderful solution. Eventually, though, the truth came out, and the truth was that Rocky's legs were broken and crushed and he had a severe bone infection. And this trauma was inflicted on a pair of legs already in terrible shape from the San Francisco accident. He was in and out of the hospital for six months as surgeons tried to add bone from other parts of his body and provide some support for his broken pins.

Cosmetically, it was a bigger disaster. Surgical scars crisscrossed his legs in all directions, joining the large zipper on his chest in a kind of macabre jigsaw puzzle. "I couldn't go to the beach or poolside anymore," said Rocky ruefully. "The scars hurt when they get too much sun, and besides, I'm a little embarrassed about it. The people in racing know who I am, but anybody who doesn't probably thinks I'm some crazy Jap who got into an auto accident or fell on a hand grenade or something."

Scares and scars. Pain when he walks, pains when he sits too long. The lingering psychological effects of two traumatic accidents. Pressure from family and friends. It's certainly more than enough to make a man give up the ghost.

So why did last November's World Offshore Powerboat Championships in Key West find Rocky riding shotgun with Al Copeland in his "Popeye" boat? "He asked me," said Rocky. Actually, the 46-foot Copeland craft was a lot easier on Rocky than the boats he used to drive. He was able to stay seated for most of the trip and thus keep the strain off his battle-scarred legs. Navigating, to the minor extent that it is needed, is not nearly as enervating as driving.

The real problem was that once Rocky climbed into the boat, heard the roar of the engines, and crossed the finish line in triumphant fashion, he felt the old fever coming back.

"I don't know whether I'll drive again," said Rocky. "My wife does not want me to. Not many of my friends want me to. And I'm not sure I want to myself. The pain in my legs might be too much. On the other hand . . ."

"If you go back to boat racing again," said Glen Simoes, "your legs will not be the issue. The issue will be your brain."

# CHAPTER

11

They were called *Fu-Go* weapons, and relatively few Americans knew about them. About 9,000 were launched from Japan near the end of World War II, 1,000 of which found their way to their intended target—the United States. The *Fu-Go* weapons, carried by hydrogen balloons, were explosives designed to detonate over various parts of the United States. The theory of the Japanese military leaders who designed them was that they would start fires, kill military men and civilians, and basically create a panic situation in the United States. Balloon warfare. Something out of H. G. Wells.

For the most part, the *Fu-Go* weapons failed. To everyone's best knowledge, they killed only six people—a woman and five children in Oregon, who were dragging one of the balloons out of the woods when it exploded—and the American press dutifully followed the army's orders not to print news of the killer balloons, thus circumventing a massive public panic. A short time later two atomic bombs rendered further development of the *Fu-Go* weapons academic.

Over twenty-five years later a Japanese man joined three Americans in another historic balloon trip. The Asian was Rocky Aoki, and the only destruction he had on his mind was the destruction of the distance record for flying a gas-filled balloon. And if he got a million dollars' worth of publicity for his Benihana restaurants in the process, so much the better.

In the two years following the near-fatal San Francisco boat crash, 1980 and 1981, Rocky needed something to satisfy his adventure quotient, and it should be clear by now that croquet was not the answer. The sport of ballooning had been on his mind for a long time, but he simply hadn't had the time to learn it. Now he did. Of course, it was not the American Medical Association-prescribed method of recuperating from heavy internal trauma, but Rocky figured, what's another life to give if you've got nine of them?

As usual, Rocky got into ballooning because someone wanted him to sponsor something. In this case, it was Paine Webber that wanted him to sponsor a hot-air balloon in the racing circuit sponsored by the investment firm. Rocky said sure, appointed himself as one member of the two-man crew, and set out to learn all he could from Tony Von Elbe, a friend who was an accomplished balloon and airplane pilot. Rocky and Von Elbe were successful on the circuit, and at one of the races they met Ben Abruzzo, who was arguably the best gas-balloon pilot in the world before the tragic plane accident that killed him, his wife, and four others in February 1985. It was a meeting that would change balloon history.

"At the time that I first met Rocky, I was thinking about flying across the continental United States," said Abruzzo. "But shortly after that Maxie Anderson and his son, Kristian, did it, so I had to think of something else." His comment gives an indication of one similarity between Abruzzo and Aoki: ". . . I had to think of something else." Abruzzo, who was a short but extraordinarily fit-looking man in his fifties, was more outwardly driven than Rocky. He was all business when he worked, and his eyes burned through you when he talked. In demeanor and effectiveness he suggested nothing less than a general, a Napoleon perhaps, which makes his eventual acceptance and even admiration of the flamboyant Rocky all the more interesting.

Abruzzo, in the spirit of one-upmanship that motivates men like him and Rocky, changed his thinking to a trans-Pacific flight. "Just like that," said Abruzzo, snapping his fingers, "Rocky said he was interested. He told me he could arrange the necessary sponsorship through Benihana and other Japanese corporations. I felt great. That was one of the major problems. I said, 'You've got a deal.'" But not in the way Abruzzo thought.

"No, you don't understand," Rocky told him. "I don't want to just sponsor you. I want to fly with you. Flying across the Pacific was one of my dreams."

Abruzzo considered this. He was not the type of man who suffered fools gently—particularly in regard to ballooning—even if they happened to be rich fools. But Abruzzo liked Rocky, and more importantly, he implicitly trusted him.

"Okay, fine," Abruzzo told him. "But I want you to understand that this isn't some fun little outing. It's a flight you may not come back from." Abruzzo wasn't blowing smoke, either. His main ballooning partner, Larry Newman, who two years earlier had accompanied Abruzzo and Maxie Anderson on a historic flight on *Double Eagle II* from Maine to France, had already told Abruzzo: "You're mad. You won't get it financed and you won't make it anyway." In June 1983 Maxie Anderson didn't make it—he died in a balloon crash in Europe. When Abruzzo died 20 months later, gas ballooning had lost its two best-known and most capable superstars.

But Rocky had no hesitation. "I'll never forget his immediate response," said Abruzzo. "He told me, 'If you're afraid to die you're afraid to live.' *That* impressed me."

Abruzzo had decided that the optimum number for the journey was three. Rocky suggested Von Elbe, but Abruzzo didn't feel that his expertise was such that it could compensate for his inability to pull his weight financially. Abruzzo wanted Newman . . . for a very good reason. "I told Rocky we needed Larry for a backup because if you lost me during the trip, you're dead. That's all—dead." Newman, despite his initial trepidation, came aboard. The challenge was too tempting.

Eventually, a fourth balloonist was taken in—Ron Clark, a real estate and former ballooning colleague of Abruzzo's in their hometown of Albuquerque. Clark had been helping Abruzzo in various organizational details of the trip and, suddenly, one day said, "I want to go with you." Abruzzo's response was typically blunt. "Why should I take you? I get calls every day from actors, musicians, singers, other balloonists, and kooks who want to go." "There's a difference," said Clark. "I'm willing to pay." Rocky, Larry, meet your new partner.

It cost Clark about $100,000 to buy in, and the eventual price tag was closer to $200,000. But Clark's contribution, like Rocky's, went far beyond finances.

"Ron was like Rocky," said Abruzzo. "He had the grit, and he stepped forward and did it. Period."

Most of the planning and training for the journey took place in Albuquerque, and the crew members took their high-altitude training at Edwards Air Force Base, using pressurized chambers to test their ability to respond to conditions of low oxygen. Rocky was blunt about his performance.

"I did lousy. I conked out so easily. What happens is that you start to get light-headed and forget what to do. You can get the oxygen, but you forget to do it while you have that 'high' feeling. But the other guys were great. They pulled me through. They were used to the altitude because they were living 5,000 feet above sea level in Albuquerque."

Actually, it was a little hairier than that. Abruzzo had decided that the best way to get Rocky some quick experience was to team with him on a series of gas balloon races. One of them was the Gordon Bennett International, in which the A team (Abruzzo and Aoki) set what was then a long-distance record by flying from Orange County, California, to Fargo, North Dakota. But not without incident. The balloonists were over 18,000 feet for almost four hours and above 21,500 for at least an hour, excessive heights that can bring about altitude sickness. They started hallucinating, Rocky espying castles and Abruzzo opting for a yellow cat that was running around the gondola. "Rocky was absolutely convinced that what he saw was real," remembered Abruzzo. "When we landed out there in the middle of nowhere, Rocky asks this farmer, 'Hey, are there any castles around here?' The guy looked at him like he was crazy."

Later, the dearth of oxygen had a more serious effect. Rocky became exhausted at one point and sat down in a corner of the gondola, his breathing increasingly shallower. "Stand up!" Captain Abruzzo shouted. "If you lay down, you're dead!" Abruzzo realized the craft was too high, but he couldn't descend because at the time they were flying above the mountains in Wyoming. A few minutes later Abruzzo saw Rocky rubbing his fingers. He looked at them and saw they were blue. "They were frostbitten at the stage where it was going to become serious damn quick," said Abruzzo. "Rubbing them was the worst thing you could do. I told him to open his parka and put his hand under his arm to warm it up. Luckily, we caught it in time."

The difficulties of the trans-Pacific flight could be itemized in a hundred different ways, but the mere fact that it took three launches to get the craft airborne says it all. The first attempt was made on

March 2, 1981. Everything was in place for takeoff when the ground wind suddenly picked up and the balloon envelope's restraining cables snapped, causing the balloon to jump out of control. The following day they tried again, but this time the capricious wind caused the balloon to drag its gondola and crew across the launch area. The flight was scrubbed, and the crew flew back to America. But the two failures may have been a blessing in disguise. *Double Eagle V* wouldn't get off the ground until eight months later, and Rocky used that time to log more valuable flight time as he and Abruzzo competed in several two-man gas balloon races. By the time *Double Eagle V* was ready for its third and what would turn out to be successful launch, Rocky had logged over 100 hours of flying, about half of those in a gas balloon, and only his crewmates and perhaps a few dozen other people in the world were as competent in the gondola. Just as he had done with wrestling, backgammon, powerboat racing, you name it, he had passed well beyond the Plimpton stage into the area of expert.

There was also some bad chemistry among the men on the first two attempts. Surprisingly, Rocky and Abruzzo, both possessed of a strong will and accustomed to calling the shots, got along splendidly—"I don't think there was ever a harsh word between us," said Abruzzo—but from the beginning Larry Newman resented the two "newcomers," particularly the flashy Aoki. Newman was, and still is, an excellent pilot, an accomplished parachutist, and a man of courage, but he was caught in a kind of nether area between captain and crewman. He was not the leader of the expedition—Abruzzo was—and though Newman was unquestionably the man to take charge if something happened to Abruzzo, it was difficult for him to be on more or less equal footing with the tenderfoots.

"We did not concentrate 100 percent on the task the first time," said Abruzzo. "I wrote a critique for the crew and made it clear there was no room for petty personality differences. There was only one goal, and that was to get across the Pacific alive and in one piece."

Though it would be misleading to indicate that Newman and Rocky and Clark ever fully worked out their differences, they made compromises and there was a new energy surrounding the third attempt. "Everything just seemed in place," said Rocky. So in place that he impulsively decided to marry Pamela the day before lift-off, November 9, in a Japanese ceremony that was a testament not only to Rocky's love but also to his promotional instincts. The Aokis could thereafter celebrate their anniversary twice—since Japan is on the other side of the international dateline, it was actually November 8 in America.

Since the mission was unique in ballooning history, it required a commensurately unique craft, and the *Double Eagle V* was it. It was an awe-inspiring affair standing thirteen stories high with a total helium capacity of 400,000 cubic feet—by comparison, *Double Eagle II,* the Abruzzo-Anderson record-setting craft, was eleven stories high with a capacity of 160,000 cubic feet. Painted on the side of the gondola was—no surprise here—a large Benihana logo, which also appeared on the crew's flight suits. On an equally grand scale was the logo of JVC, a huge Japanese audio-video company from whom Rocky had procured sponsorship of $600,000. Another sponsor was the Japanese beer company, Kirin, whose executives would later be crying into their beer with joy when Rocky succeeded in placing Kirin beer bottles in front of the ABC cameras during a conversation with Ted Koppel on *Nightline.* Altogether, Rocky raised about $1.2 million for the project. He sold the American television rights to ABC for about $200,000, the Japanese television rights for $100,000, and the in-flight photo rights to *National Geographic* for $50,000. Benihana ended up spending about $250,000 on the project, but Rocky estimates that he recouped that three times over in publicity. (But then, what else would he say?)

Dipping into his bottomless pit of contacts, Rocky had arranged for the crew and their families to stay at a resort owned by a friend in Nagashima, a city about 200 miles southwest of Tokyo. The launch would be made from there so the proprietor could benefit from the publicity. For that he provided about $150,000 in the way of free food, lodging, laundry, and equipment to the balloonists. Also, Rocky had arranged for his good friend, Flip Wilson, to fly to Nagashima to sing "The Star-Spangled Banner" for the launch. And as a counterpart, Rocky invited Japan's best-known traditional (enka) singer, a man named Masao Sen, to offer a Japanese song.

Since Japanese aviation authorities were concerned about the crowded afternoon airspace over Tokyo International Airport, liftoff was scheduled for the ungodly hour of 3:05 a.m. And even that wasn't a fait accompli. No matter how carefully a ballooning team plans its trip, it is still a slave to the weather, and *Double Eagle V*'s weather crew said that was the ideal time to go. It cannot be stated strongly enough that on such a long journey the balloonists are, to a certain extent, in the hands of God. They can plot their courses and keep in touch with the ground crew all they want, but they have to depend on a certain measure of providence for a safe journey. As it turned out, this flight would need a large measure of providence.

There were other, more pragmatic concerns that made this a dangerous flight. Since there was not another four-man balloon in existence, and since it was too great a financial risk to fly *Double Eagle V* before the actual launch, the four-man crew was essentially going at it cold, with no warm-up. Whatever would go wrong would be going wrong for the first time. And there were the human considerations. Four men cast adrift in a sometimes hostile environment, needing each other yet needing to make quick, strategic decisions, sometimes added up to a rather charged atmosphere. And making the atmosphere even more charged was the specter of Rocky as human lightning rod.

Several physicians had advised him against making the trip because of the steel rod that was implanted in his leg as a result of the San Francisco accident (it's since been removed). "At 20,000 feet," said Rocky, "I would become quite attractive to lightning."

As is the case with most balloon expeditions, there was an overwhelming air of uncertainty enveloping the project. Balloonists have to take advantage of prevailing conditions, and no one knows exactly what condition will be prevailing in the future. The crew knew only that it wanted to fly all the way across the Pacific from land mass to land mass. That was of particular importance. There had been much dispute in ballooning circles about whether Maxie and Kristian Anderson had actually completed a transcontinental flight since they had not landed near the Atlantic Ocean, and the *Double Eagle V* crew didn't want any questions about their journey. But once they crossed the Pacific, their intention was to keep going for as long as possible, all the way around the world, the Fates permitting. Though no one truly believed that would happen, Abruzzo did feel that they had a decent chance of crossing the United States and the Atlantic Ocean and landing in Europe. To that end Abruzzo had brought along charts for the entire Northern Hemisphere.

Only one crewman expressed no desire to go to Europe—Larry Newman. "Fine," Abruzzo told him, "I'll give you a chute and a backup and jump. Adios. It would've been a helluva publicity number, too. 'Crewman Decides to Jump out over New York City.' But I know Larry—he would've changed his mind and gone on with us." In all likelihood, it would have been Rocky who grabbed the chute and seized the publicity initiative.

*Double Eagle V*'s journey was all the more perilous because it was to be completely over water. If something goes wrong over land, chances are a crew can make a few adjustments and have a reasonable chance at a safe landing; if something goes wrong in the middle of the Pacific, chances are a crew will drown. Abruzzo explained further.

"The theory when flying over water is that if you have trouble or the balloon ruptures, you bail out, open the chute, then, as you get close to the water, deploy your raft. And when you see the raft touch the water—and no sooner!—you reach for the quick-release on your chute and land on the raft before the chute drags you under and drowns you.

"Now, how hard would that be to accomplish? What are your chances of being rescued? Well, I'll tell you. Halfway across the Pacific, Rocky was dickering around with his belly-pack parachute. 'I'm trying to figure out how this hooks up,' he told me. 'Here, let me help you,' I said. And I threw the thing out of the balloon. 'What are you doing?' he said. I said, 'Well, there's another procedure. You throw the raft out and try to land on it because you have about as much chance that way.'" So much for the possibility of a dramatic water landing.

Any thoughts that this would be a trouble-free flight were taken away immediately when *Double Eagle V* lifted off and headed, not for the jet stream, but for a nearby seawall. The balloon struck a cherry tree, lodged there for a moment, then twisted away toward the seawall again. The crew frantically started dumping ballast, an omen for the entire journey. Over 400 pounds of sand and a 130-pound oxygen tank had to be dumped before the gondola lifted off into the wild blue yonder. Later, the cherry tree would be repaired and renamed by the shrine-conscious Japanese as "The Rocky Tree."

"What I remember most clearly about the whole trip, I think, were the lights over Nagashima," said Rocky. "They were beautiful when we took off, just like when you look out the window of a plane over a big city. Then they got dimmer and dimmer, taking us farther and farther away. We could be getting off on a great journey, or we could be heading toward our deaths. Many men had died traveling less distance than we were going."

Each of the crew members had specific duties during the expedition: Rocky, for example, was in charge of operating the video cameras and taking the other photographs "since I was the Japanese guy." Theoretically, they were to navigate in two-man shifts while the other two slept in sleeping bags on the floor of the gondola (temperatures dipped to minus ten degrees Fahrenheit at night), but from the beginning there was a lot more extra work to be done than they had planned. One of the basic problems was that the balloon was inadvertently underinflated by 6 percent, a condition that prevented the craft from achieving the initial climb altitude Abruzzo wanted. This caused *Double Eagle V* to pick up ice from a cascading of airs. At one time there was as much as three tons of ice lying on top of the balloon, creating, in effect, a pushing-down motion on the craft. The balloon changed altitudes constantly, taking the crew on what resembled a giant department-store elevator ride rather than a tranquil, free-floating journey. At one point late in the flight, *Double Eagle V* sank to 4,200 feet, "so low," remembers Rocky, "that we could see the ocean." It was a constant struggle to throw over enough ballast to enable the craft to climb to a higher altitude. Aside from that, it was a numbingly elemental journey—four men flying, sometimes blindly, across a vast expanse of ocean. They saw only one craft on their four-day journey—a liquid petroleum tanker with which they tried to make contact with their marine radio. The LPT either never picked up the signal or simply ignored them.

As the balloon reached the California coast, it was apparent that this would not be the ambitious nearly-around-the-world trip Abruzzo had wanted. The battle with the ice had simply taken too much ballast, and *Double Eagle V* was losing altitude. At one point it appeared they were heading for the Golden Gate Bridge. "If we can nail this one," Abruzzo told the crew, "it will be the most spectacular landing in history." Double spectacular for Rocky, who would have gone into the books as the only man ever to crash in the San Francisco Bay both by sea and by air.

Alas, it was not to be. The craft drifted northward. Night was falling. The best plan would have been to keep going until the following day to maximize publicity—"No pictures at night, you know," noted Rocky—but that would have involved climbing above the Sierras. "We simply wouldn't have made it," said Abruzzo. To make the situation all but impossible, instead of merely extremely dangerous, the worst storm in two decades was pounding the Northern California coast. "Everything," said Abruzzo, "was turning to crap." He presented his options to the crew:

"I haven't taken a vote on anything yet, but I think we should consider our options together. If we land now, the seas are running ten to fifteen feet. We have good separation. A water landing is a piece of cake. We're going to come away in one piece, but we will *not* have made it from one land mass to another. We'll be one hundred, two hundred yards, a mile short.

"Now, if we go on, we've got zero-zero conditions—zero visibility, zero separation. We've got high winds. We've got a raging storm. We're going to fly into mountains, and if we get lucky, we can maybe find a reasonably level place, but it's going to be a tough, tough landing. The chances are fifty-fifty. I'd like to hear from each of you." And one by one, Rocky, Ron and Larry all said: "I'm in. Let's go for land."

An initial landing attempt near the town of Willits was a near-disaster—*Double Eagle V* dropped to 500 feet before the men realized they were on a collision course with a row of houses. Could they really have expected anything different with disaster-prone Rocky aboard? They decided to try a valley near the town of Covelo, which lies about 170 miles north of San Francisco. As a final test, the craft narrowly missed crashing into a mountain—the men had to throw out almost all their remaining ballast, including a $10,000 video camera, to rise above it—and finally slammed into the Mount San Hedrin hillside. The gondola was perched at a precarious angle, and only the presence of tough manzanita brush at the top of the mountain kept the gondola from tumbling down the mountainside.

Naturally, they were happy to be alive, but it was a somewhat ignoble landing. There had been events of epic grandeur during the trip that they hadn't even realized—such as the gathering of throngs of people on the ground who were looking skyward and cheering them on, or the time the attendant on a Japan Airlines flight announced to the passengers: "Mr. Rocky Aoki is flying his balloon at this same altitude"—but here they were on a mountainside near some town they had never heard of, sprawled in a heap at the back of a gondola. Ground control at Oakland made almost immediate contact with them, but Abruzzo said not to bother sending a search party in the darkness. So they spent the final hours of their five-night, four-day journey "camping out" in their gondola.

Whatever the others were thinking, Rocky was thinking about how to maximize his ink. When daylight broke and rescue helicopters arrived at the top of the mountain, Rocky put a Benihana flag—he just happened to have one handy—in the gondola. He instructed the other crew members not to talk about their experience but to wait until the multitudes had gathered at his Benihana restaurant in San Francisco, where they would meet the press for the first time. They did agree to talk to schoolchildren in Covelo in the morning before flying to Benihana, where, not surprisingly, Rocky held center stage during the press conference.

Ballooning, hot-air and gas, is pretty much out of Rocky's blood now, just as backgammon, antique collecting, car collecting, and any one of a dozen other things are. But he would climb in the gondola again if the stakes were high enough.

"What really interested me for a while was getting the Russian government to cooperate in a ballooning project," says Rocky. "Maybe we could get a Russian cosmonaut or somebody else famous to represent that country, and get Ben from the United States and get me from Japan and make a flight for peace or something." It probably won't happen. Before his death, Abruzzo had pursued the project with the Russian authorities until he finally reached the ambassador.

"He finally told me, very formally: 'Mr. Abruzzo, if you insist on flying over our country, we will have to shoot you down.'" The exclamation point in Abruzzo's mind came along a few months later when the Russians shot down a Korean airliner.

Whatever else Rocky got out of the trip—publicity for Benihana, a personal longing for adventure, a few more bumps and bruises on the pin cushion he calls his body—he got the enduring respect of Abruzzo. His participation in *Double Eagle V* was just another indication that he has the right stuff.

"If I were to make another flight, I would take Rocky in place of a more experienced gas balloonist. I'm not saying I'd fly a mission with him that required two of me—he still needs more experience in areas like meteorology and navigation—but if you just needed guys with true grit, you'd want to get guys like Rocky and Ron Clark. These guys are not afraid of anything. They were like animals. If they had fear, I didn't see it. On the landing, when it was obvious we could've been killed, they performed in a manner that is hard to describe. They did everything by the numbers; they did it well; they didn't desert their posts for a second."

"The same can be said of Ben," said Rocky. "He was a brave man, a risk-taker, yes, but a man who always knew what he was doing."

The intrepid crew of *Double Eagle V, from left to right,* Larry Newman, Ben Abruzzo, Rocky, and Ron Clark, standing before the permanent exhibit in the Smithsonian's Air and Space Museum. Abruzzo, the captain on the flight, was killed in a plane crash in February 1985.

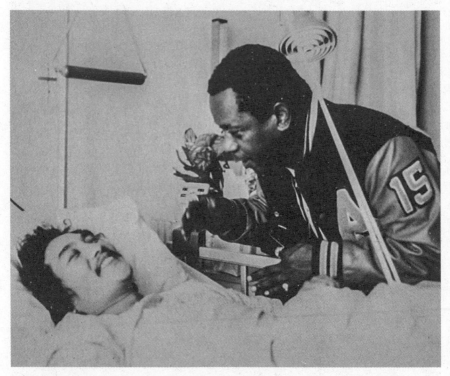

Following the near-fatal boat crash in San Francisco Bay in 1979, Rocky's close friend Flip Wilson made a bedside request: "Please quit racing." "Stuff it," Rocky murmured.

Rocky's next adventure would take him to record depths—below the ocean, that is. Here, with facility director Roger Cook of the Harbor Branch Foundation in Florida, Rocky enjoys some time out after a test drive in the exotic two-man submersible.

Rocky hangs out with fans and members of the US Air Force's precision flying team, Blue Angels. The following morning, he went out and won the Benihana Offshore Grand Prix Powerboat Race.

Rocky with Bernie Kopell of *Love Boat* fame.

Despite having myriad interests and hobbies, Rocky still found time to brainstorm new projects with his management team.

Twenty years of intensive promotion of the Benihana name on boats, balloons, and cars started to pay off. They were like giant advertising billboards, said Rocky. When he introduced a new line of frozen foods in 1984, the public's response to the Benihana brand was overwhelming.

Japan's powerboat racing czar, Tadashi Sasakawa, wishes Rocky luck before a race. The two once planned a Benihana hotel/casino in Atlantic City, but financial and construction pitfalls doomed the project.

# CHAPTER

12

ast year a well-heeled Junior Chamber of Commerce in the
Fukuoka Prefecture on the Japanese island of Kyushu had two
choices for its annual speaker at a three-day conference: Henry
Kissinger and Rocky Aoki. They chose Aoki. Which tells you all you
need to know about the regard with which Rocky is held back in his
native Japan.

"He's a national celebrity," says Pam Aoki. "He's treated like he's
one of their boys who went out into the world and did very well.
Which is exactly what he is."

"The Japanese don't mob their heroes like we do over here," says
Aoki's close friend and fellow adventurer, Pierre John Leo Bonnescuelle
de Lespinois (no kidding). "But I've been to Japan with him, and he's
like Robert Redford. That's the only thing I can compare it to."

But what is the converse of that? What does Rocky think of the
country he left behind twenty-five years ago? Which Japanese per-
sona has he retained, and which has he discarded? To which nation,
ultimately, will Rocky pledge his heart and soul?

"All the stuff about Rocky as a Horatio Alger guy, all the rags-to-riches stuff is relevant," said Glen Simoes. "But the real interesting thing about Rocky is the way he lives in two worlds, this 'man of two cultures' thing. If you can unlock that, you'd have the key to unlocking Rocky. Not that that's a simple thing, of course."

The simple thing is to proclaim Rocky "Americanized" and leave it at that. And indeed, there's a large measure of truth to it. It's the first thing an American, John Mandel, says about him, and it's the first thing a fellow Asian, Henry Look, says about him. Quite often it's the first thing Rocky says about himself in casual conversation. And there's a lot of truth to it. But there's a lot of Japan, too, in this expatriate from the Land of the Rising Sun.

To begin with, there is a precedent in Japanese society for the personality type that fits the young Hiroaki Aoki. Bernard Rudofsky, author of *The Kimono Mind*, calls it "the honorable brat," and points out that there is a kind of grudging admiration for this person. Rocky certainly fit that mold, with the wise-guy street fighting and the privileges of *bancho*. Though Rocky's father sometimes battled with him over his adolescent transgressions, and his mother sometimes despaired after her trips to meet with the authorities at Keio, Rocky was never really made to feel anything but special as a kid. His actions were tolerated because he was *chonan*, his aggressiveness accepted because of his intelligence. "I was a top guy," said Rocky, "and I knew it." The difference, of course, is that most Japanese gentlemen of Rocky's generation grew out of their "honorable brat" stage and became, in the best Japanese tradition, team players. Rocky did not. There's still a lot of the honorable brat about him.

There is also a place in the Japanese character that accounts for Rocky's frenetic switching from one thing to another. The Japanese word is *imamekashi*, meaning passion for the newest thing. "The ardent pursuit of a hobby," wrote Reischauer in *The Japanese*, "is almost necessary for self-respect in Japan." Of course, the average Japanese simply does not have the resources to pick up on the expensive hobbies that Rocky does, but the character trait is nevertheless consistent.

This obsessive switching from one thing to another suggests a herd instinct to the Japanese. And not even the most fervent Nipponophile would deny that if you have a thousand Japanese in a crowd with cameras around their necks, you don't have a thousand photographers as much as you have a large picture-taking school of fish. The Italian writer, Maraini, stated this point eloquently when he wrote, "One of the things which strikes foreigners, particularly Latins, most vividly is that when you meet the Japanese you rarely have the impression of meeting an outstanding personality, with an above-average intelligence, though when you meet Japan (the product of some labour, a work of art, an event) you are so often carried away by the warmest admiration."

It is at this point that Rocky diverges from his countrymen. With a vengeance. Rocky has never had a problem being a "personality." He does not fade into the background, camera around his neck, but rather tends to stay in sharp focus. Part of it is a natural charisma, the legacy of Yunosuke Aoki, the old showman. If there was one area of comparison between Rocky and his father, it was their ability to attract and hold a crowd. Rocky's other drawing card has been the very "Americanism" that everyone talks about. He is open, outgoing, and friendly, qualities not normally associated with Japanese. Therefore, he surprises people, catching them off-guard. Conditioned to fight through a wall of Asian reticence, Americans meeting Rocky for the first time instead find a smiling, warm, open-door of a man. Rocky scores points for merely being friendly. Another aspect of Rocky's attraction to people, of course, has been his power and wealth. But that came later. The attraction of his personality, the charisma and magnetism, were a priori to his success as a moneymaker. The luminosity of his personality, in contrast to the grayness of most of his countrymen, is perhaps the greatest area of divergence between Rocky and his birthright.

At the same time, however, a distinctively Japanese aspect to Rocky's personality is evident at times. Yes, Rocky does flamboyant things but he doesn't always do them flamboyantly, powerboat crashes notwithstanding. There's a sense of control about the man, something akin to what the Japanese call *enryo*, which means "reserve" or "constraint." Not long ago an observer watched Rocky glad-hand his way through a cocktail party, stopping to talk to one group for a minute only to be beckoned to another. "I don't know, he seems so—so controlled for somebody who does so much," she said.

Sometimes it goes beyond *enryo*. Remember Tad Suga, so overcome by Rocky's outward flamboyance, so surprised by the inward shyness he came to know? Pamela Aoki sees the same thing at times. "Rocky is very comfortable with small groups of people, but put him in a room with a large group and he does not enjoy himself. Most people would think that he'd be in his element at large parties, but he really doesn't enjoy them. I remember we had a big Christmas party down in Miami a few years ago, and Rocky spent the whole time hidden away in a corner. I can still see him standing there. A lot of people thought it odd, but I really wasn't surprised."

Another obvious Japanese aspect of Rocky's personality is his strong willpower, his resolve. It steeled him in the early lonely months at the first Benihana; it secured him as he beat the odds by expanding his restaurant concept faster than five-minute rice; it saved him when he lay near death in San Francisco Bay. Not that the Japanese have a monopoly on willpower, but it is a quality that is pervasive in their national character. Remember Lieutenant Onoda, who for a quarter century held out in his solitary battle with America on a Philippine island? It is not hard to imagine Rocky exercising a similar act of will, except that he would have waited twenty-five years for a camera crew to arrive.

A companion characteristic is the surface emotionlessness of the Japanese male. No matter how much pain he feels inside, he considers it a sign of weakness to show it. It's not quite as cut-and-dried as that, of course, but the Asian man is nowhere nearly as free with his emotions as the Latin or even the American. It might figure that, since Rocky is a much freer spirit than his countrymen, he would not have this clamp on his feelings. But he does. Chizuru felt it strongly after she lost their first child. "Rocky made no response to it at all," said Chizuru. "I just couldn't figure it out. It made me feel so bad. But, you know, later on, one of his chefs told me they heard Rocky yelling and crying with grief while he was alone in the shower. He felt it but he couldn't show me."

She remembers another incident. One of his brothers, Hiro, met Rocky at Kennedy Airport. Hiro was crying with joy because he hadn't seen his brother in several years. "I still remember Rocky looking bewildered because his brother was crying. 'What's the matter,' he said, 'does he have a stomach ache or something?' Now, maybe he cares deep inside. I don't know. I really don't know."

"I remember that day well," said Rocky. "Hiro, he was glad to see me but at that time I couldn't identify with that. Maybe I was too busy then, trying to establish myself and my business. I didn't even think about emotion or what he might be feeling.

"Now, it would be different. I'm actually a very emotional person. I cry at movies all the time. But, still, I want to hide. I don't want people to see me crying. I still think of it as a weakness."

Few aspects of Japanese life are as striking to the American as the relationship between men and women, or more precisely, between husband and wife. It is evolving, of course, just as it is in America, but it is still extremely chauvinistic. "In Japan a wife is not supposed to ask for anything," says Chizuru Aoki. "It was okay to say you wanted something if somebody asked you. But otherwise, a wife is supposed to be like this couch I'm sitting on."

Rocky struggles with the disparate views of marriage from the two societies. Not that American chauvinists are exactly an endangered species, of course, but Rocky has run smack into the brick wall of feminism in the person of Pamela Aoki. In the abstract there is no doubt Rocky believes in the Japanese way. As he looks at it, he's done his job as a breadwinner, and in a perfect world a wife would stay home and do hers.

"I have trouble with Pamela that way," says Rocky. "She doesn't always want to stay home and take care of the kids. Now, in my way, the Japanese way, I go out and make money, make deals, play around, whatever. My first wife believed in that [though not to the degree that Rocky might have thought].

"The way I see it, the kids will be smarter if the wife stays home and teaches them. That's how it was for me back in Japan. My mother taught me. The husband doesn't have to be smart if the mother is smart."

That, of course, is Rocky's side of the story. Pamela Aoki has a different one. About the only concession Pam will make on her husband's sense of marital equality is that Rocky "has improved." Particularly in his understanding of time. A common misconception about the Japanese is that they are slavishly punctual, virtual automatons who march to the ticking of a clock. Well, perhaps in the business world, but not in the social world. Visitors to Japan are often surprised when parties and informal gatherings just can't seem to get themselves going on time. Neither can Rocky.

"Being a sort of precise person, I'd just get driven nuts by Rocky in the beginning of our relationship because he'd be like four and five hours late for a date," says Pam. "Now, that's sort of unheard of, right, to be that late? And then he used to walk in like nothing happened. His feeling was, 'I'm here now. What's the problem?' Not even a phone call.

"Now I could understand it a little bit. I tried to realize how harassed he might've been that day and be understanding. I wanted him to be able to relax when he was with me.

"I just gradually learned how to deal with it. I never, ever depended on him. If I had something to do around the house while I was waiting for him, I just went ahead and did it and didn't think about how late he was. Or if I was meeting him out someplace, I'd have a backup plan. Like, 'Okay, I'll meet you someplace at five, but if you're not there, call this number at seven, or if you don't do that, I'll meet you at this place at ten.' It's gotten so it works out as long as I plan on the unexpected."

The unexpected was exactly what Pam got on the day that Rocky finally proposed. Well, not completely unexpected. What he did was call Pam up from Japan, where he was preparing for the trans-Pacific balloon flight, and said: "Pam, could you come over two days early?" "Rocky, that's tomorrow." "I know," he said. So she went to pack. One of Rocky's friends met her at the airport with a large bouquet. "Congratulations," he said. "For what?" said Pam. "You're getting married." "Oh," she said. Another milestone in romantic history.

Rocky had decided he wanted a traditional Japanese Shinto ceremony. Everyone remembers the beauty of the ceremony, and certainly it was one of the few weddings in history to be filmed by *The American Sportsman*, the network show that was carrying the balloon flight.

And what does Rocky remember about the big day? "I remember how nice Pamela looked in a kimono," he said.

But how much of Rocky's desire for a traditional Japanese wedding was hype and how much was sincere? As always with Rocky, the question is difficult to answer. But his feelings about his native land are complex in a way that they were not when he left it twenty-five years ago, and they're still evolving.

No one understands them better than a fellow native like Tad Suga, who, like Rocky, left Japan for the promised land and is only now beginning to realize what he left behind.

"I know that when Rocky first came over, he tried to forget he was Japanese," said Suga, "because I did the same thing. You know, the first three years I was here, I didn't read one newspaper or magazine from Japan. Now? I ask them to send me everything. I remember something that made an impression on me here. I was watching a Danny Kaye comedy—he was a pirate or something—and somebody pulled off his arm, and he said, 'Oh, made in Japan, I guess.'

"I thought, 'Oh, so that's what they think of us.' Japan was a joke. But today it's cameras, TVs, cars, watches from Japan. It has made it easier for us." His feelings for Japan have changed so much that Suga, the man who didn't pick up a Japanese publication for three years, is considering going back there to live some day.

Rocky sorted through the same complicated feelings about Japan. He avoided "made in Japan" with the same zealousness that he avoided "icky, slimy things" in his restaurant. Significantly, so did his father, a man who assiduously pursued traditional Japanese construction in the Benihana restaurants and sometimes regaled his son with tales of the samurai.

"All my father's clothes were bought in England and Italy. It was like that with everything. But if he was around today, he'd do the same thing I do. I'm looking all the time for 'Made in Japan.' I pick something up in a store, and if it was made in Japan I buy it, even if I don't always need it."

There's a suggestion of front runner in Rocky's opinions on Japan. He wanted nothing to do with it before, but now that it's become a world economic power, he's back on the bandwagon. Suga even says that Rocky treats Japanese customers differently these days. "It may have been my imagination but I never thought Rocky paid any attention to the Japanese customers before. Now, it's different. They do business with each other. He's on their level; they're on his."

If that is true, then it's also true that Rocky has never been hypocritical in his views on Japan. The things he found wrong with the country two decades ago he still finds wrong with it—the lack of entrepreneurialism, the rewarding of experience over talent, the sacrifice of individuality. And he doesn't hesitate to tell them about it, either. He hammers away at the theme of individuality in his frequent speeches in Japan, and he gets cheered loud and long at each stop. "You see, everybody in Japan wants to follow Rocky, but they can't," says Aki Sato, a Japanese businessman in San Francisco. "It's that simple."

Even with all the impact that Japan has made in the civilized world, its individual personality remains elusive. Rocky is an anomaly. There is Rocky, and there are the Japanese people, and never, seemingly, shall the twain meet. Sometimes it's a source of frustration for Rocky.

"I'm in a cocktail lounge in San Francisco a while ago, and this Korean guy comes up to me and starts talking to me in Korean. 'Sorry, I don't speak that,' I told him. So he does it again. 'Look,' I said, 'English or Japanese. That's all.' And he says in English, 'Hey, don't put down Korea. Don't underestimate your country.' I tell him, 'Hey, chief, I am Japanese.' 'You cannot be Japanese,' he says to me. 'I know you are Korean.' Then he walks away. It's happened to me several other times, too."

Obviously, Rocky is something special in Japan, particularly to the younger generation, which has tracked his adventuresome exploits more than his business successes. "Young people come up to me every week and just want to talk about Rocky," says his mother back in Japan. That is understandable since the generation that followed Rocky was really the first to question the groupthink mentality of their forefathers and draw on *shutaisei,* which roughly translates into "subjectivity," or the sense of being the active subject rather than the passive object in one's life.

But there's also that grudging respect that Rocky has from his peer group, which, as Sato says, wants to follow Rocky but can't. Indeed, it is an older generation of Japanese that has asked Rocky to run as a candidate for senator back in the Old Country.

"I considered it seriously," says Rocky. "The campaign could have been financed by Benihana in Japan for a couple of million, and my backers were willing to let me basically run my business over here and come to Japan maybe four or five times a year. But I didn't think it would be fair to the people. It wasn't giving enough of my time."

The whole package seems to add up rather nicely for a storybook life back in Japan for the Aokis. Pamela would make an excellent Jackie for this politician of Kennedyesque appeal. And after his term of service has concluded, he and his family could retire comfortably to the huge ranch the family owns in Chiba, a town about thirty miles from Tokyo.

But in all likelihood it won't come to pass.

"Rocky has never taken on American citizenship, and that says something to me," says Pam. "I know that he feels very proud of the accomplishments of his country. But, still, he's different. Everything over there is set, and Rocky is not set. The great thing they have is teamwork, and Rocky never really cared for teamwork. Over there you don't see any young executives. It's not the ability of the man; it's the procedure."

"And if there's one thing I'm not," says Rocky, "is a man of procedure."

# CHAPTER

13

A few months before Rocky was to open his first Benihana at the unpromising site of the old Bamboo House, a friend named Donald Karas, who was in the magazine publishing business, showed up with a distinguished visitor. He was George Eng, a successful restaurateur who had already opened several Chinese restaurants in Atlanta. Karas wanted him to look at Rocky's concept as a possible investment. Karas knew that Eng would consider Rocky an unknown but felt he might see the same sort of spark in him that Karas had seen.

"My motive was to get involved financially through Eng if he thought it would work," remembers Karas. "They had a talk and Eng was unimpressed. Finally, his message to Rocky was this: 'Hey, I'm George Eng. I'm a great restaurateur. What do I need you for?' And he left." Something he would have hardly done today.

Rocky sits atop an empire that, so it seems, can only grow. His restaurants produce about $75 million a year. He owns just under 60 percent of the stock in Benihana National Corporation, his first public venture. All future restaurant expansion in the United States, as well as Benihana's frozen food line (which Rocky thinks will become a $100 million business) will be under the aegis of BNC. He has as yet untapped resources in Japan, where the Aoki family owns Benihana Company, Limited, a business that grosses between $50 and $60 million. For years Rocky has owned only 17 percent—the majority (about 70 percent) is owned by Yasuhiro's widow and Hiro—but at the end of 1984 he was considering an offer from his mother to become president and chairman of the board. That would mean another $200,000 in salary and, given the Rocky magic, a substantial increase in revenues for the whole operation.

All in all, things are looking rosy for Rocky the businessman. Here's a closer look.

It is difficult to classify Benihana restaurants. Are they in the ethnic food class? Yes, to a certain extent, but the basic Big Three that Rocky took to twenty-one years ago—beef, chicken, shrimp—are familiar to American diners. Are they in the fast-food class? Yes, to a certain extent, but the term doesn't do justice to the excellent taste of the fare. Yes, it's cooked quickly, but it's also made fresh to order, in front of your eyes. That's why it's not exactly accurate, either, to classify it with the "chain" restaurants that have so dotted the American landscape since the late 1950s—quite simply, it has better food than most of them.

"It's easiest to categorize Benihana by categorizing Rocky," says Karas. "I put Rocky in that class of entrepreneurial restaurateurs who changed the eating habits of America. Almost every one of these guys started in the late fifties, early sixties. Before that the only thing close in concept was the automats. Now, they've almost completely died out.

"Rocky is right up there with people like Ray Kroc of McDonald's and John Y. Brown of Kentucky Fried Chicken. He may not get the publicity or notoriety that they do within the business, but he's their equal. That's the level I put him on."

It is extraordinary that Rocky was able to expand in McDonald's-like fashion in the early 1970s without franchising (except, as mentioned earlier, for the few franchises that did make it). There's no single reason he was able to do it, of course, but one factor is inescapable: he took the expansion risk where the others would not. One day last year Rocky sat in Benihana West on 56th Street in New York City, looked out the window, and proclaimed: "Look at all those restaurants out there. Some of them do better than I do here, some do worse. But they all could've been where I am *if* they were willing to take a chance."

Rocky took chances, but he made plans, too. At each stop along the restaurant trail from New York City to Hawaii he firmly believed that his concept would go once he got people in the front door to watch the chefs, smell the aroma of cooking food, and eat his steak. But he also knew how to get people in the front door.

"By and large, there's nothing different between our restaurant and another new guy opening on the street," says Bill Susha, Benihana's assistant to the president. "We had the same problems, the same everything. But we might've been a little more promotion-conscious in those days. No, I don't mean a little; I mean a lot.

"We'd bombard an area. We had our own public relations people working, of course, but we'd usually hire someone locally, too. That helped a lot because that person knew the area. We'd invite the right local celebrities. Rocky's friend, Flip Wilson [who paid all his own expenses as a token of his friendship to Rocky], was at quite a lot of our openings. A lot of restaurants would just have hors d'oeuvres to eat, but we'd serve the whole menu with maybe three seatings. Yes, it did cost a lot of money but that's what Rocky believed in, and ultimately, he was usually proven right."

What Rocky really knew how to do was create an event. The celebrities would attract the social publicity, the food would attract the dining-out publicity, and the Shinto priest that he imported from the West Coast to bless the new restaurant would attract the feature publicity.

"In those early days," says Susha, "there really was a conscious effort to introduce some Japanese culture to America, to familiarize America to Japan through the restaurant. The priest, the construction, the artifacts on the walls, the politeness of the employees—all that really helped us do that. And it was part of our success."

After people like Susha and Simoes came aboard in 1970, Benihana used some demographics to determine its sites, rather than rely on Rocky's instincts. They determined, for example, that by and large their customers were not the blue-collar crowd that might want a salad bar and piped-in muzak rather than, say, a Shinto priest and showy chefs. They looked to cities that were sophisticated, cities that had a lot of transplanted New Yorkers, such as Atlanta (opened May 10, 1974) and Bethesda, Maryland (opened October 25, 1974). Even with the control of his staff, Rocky wanted to move fast. "His goal back then might be roughly described as wanting to open a restaurant every month in every area of the country," says Susha, smiling. It wasn't always that simple to find a deal. Even the conservative Susha, for example, was convinced that the rapidly growing Atlanta market could sustain two Benihanas back in the 1970s. Hindsight proves him correct. But Rocky couldn't find the right deal, and consequently, Atlanta II didn't open until April 26, 1981.

And there were just plain misses. At the end of 1984, three restaurants in the chain were either losing money or at the break-even point—New Orleans, Salt Lake City, and Cherry Hill, New Jersey. New Orleans opened early in 1977 in the French Quarter, which meant it had to compete with Antoine's, The Court of the Two Sisters, and all the rest. Rocky and his people found that when people came to the French Quarter, they were going for French food, not

Japanese. If Benihana had opened in a New Orleans suburb, it might have done very well. As of last year Rocky's people were looking into the idea of changing the concept to a jazz club or something along that line.

Salt Lake City, which opened in April 1977, is an example showing that even Rocky can have bad luck. The city boasts a large Japanese-American population from the World War II internment camps, and Rocky located the restaurant directly across the street from a beehive of activity, the Salt Palace. Alas, Benihana got caught in a redevelopment project that placed another structure in front of Benihana. Also, Rocky and his staff had underestimated the Mormon influence in Utah. For every Japanese-American who makes his way to Benihana, there are ten Mormons staying home to take care of the kids.

Neither Rocky nor anybody else can figure out what happened in Cherry Hill, which opened on February 14, 1978. It just never took off. But the lease on the restaurant doesn't expire until the year 2003, and it's a safe bet that Cherry Hill will remain in the chain. Why? Because that's how Rocky and his people like to do business.

"In a strictly American company I think you would've seen these restaurants disposed of," says Susha. "There is a bottom line concept to everything, and frankly, these three aren't making it. But we don't look at it like that for two reasons. First, we're pretty tenacious in wanting to make something work. Secondly, there's the family nature of the operation. There's still a certain paternalism that exists from the old days when this was a family operation."

A true Japanese might not be as impressed by that paternalism. Nick Kobayashi, Rocky's brother-in-law and his vice-president of operations, remembers with fondness the old days back at Benihana East when the waitresses used to brew him soup when he was sick. "These days you don't see it," says Kobayashi, "the reason being that there's so many more Americans working at Benihanas."

On the other hand, Kobayashi may not be as familiar with the basically cutthroat nature of American business. If the bottom line isn't there, the shop is closed down and it doesn't matter much where the bodies are stacked. Rocky doesn't operate that way. "Everybody who works for me wants to grow," he says. "If they don't want to grow, I don't want them. I understand the feeling because I always wanted to grow, to better myself. The waitress wants to become assistant manager; the assistant manager wants to become a manager. What happens to them if I just close down a place and leave them deserted?" In this respect Rocky is halfway between traditional American and traditional Japanese: he will fire an employee in a minute if he's not doing his job, which happens infrequently in Japan, but he'll go to the wire to save a job if the person has been loyal, which isn't always the case in corporate America.

There is also the other quality Susha mentioned—tenacity. "Rocky does not like to lose a restaurant," says Al Geduldig. "He considers it a personal defeat if something goes under." Susha remembers the moment when Rocky decided he simply had to close down the franchise in Puerto Rico where his friend was serving corned beef sandwiches. "Rocky and all of us somehow felt that there would be a tremendous negative effect when people saw the Benihana sign come down. We all felt it strongly. In retrospect, it was better that we did it, of course, but I think some of that feeling remains, the feeling that we should stick with something and try to make it work." But it's not done to the point of absurdity. Late in 1984 Rocky was forced to close the Palace in New York City, once the gemstone of the Benihana display case. Business was good, but the landlord, in a power play to try and increase his profits, asked for a lease of close to $200,000 per year, an increase of about 300 percent. Rocky said no. The Palace is closed forever, and the memory of it moves even Rocky to true emotion.

"I feel very bad because of my father. The trouble he went to build that restaurant was unbelievable. He went to the top of a mountain in Japan to get the old farmhouse, then dragged the pieces through the snow with a horse. The whole process took over two years. So much time he put into that place, so much time."

Other changes in the business have become necessary. "After twenty years people get bored with the same thing all the time," says Susha, "and no one is more attuned to that fact than Rocky." Actually, even in the boom-boom years Rocky had never been satisfied with Benihana's net profit (he is quick to acknowledge, however, that his own personal forays had something to do with the bottom line), and the corporation's profits in 1982 slipped 20 percent from the year before, a consequential margin in any business. The dip caused Benihana to run some promotions that had previously been considered, in the words of Glen Simoes, "anathema," and to try a few experimentations with the previously sancrosanct Big Three of beef, chicken, and shrimp.

In certain selected local markets there had always been slight variations on the menu. Out in Hawaii, for example, a customer could get *mahi-mahi*. The original franchisee in Miami and Fort Lauderdale had—stupidly it seemed—put chicken livers on the menu. But after Rocky bought the restaurants back and removed chicken livers from the menu, he found the demand for them still existed from the regular customers. So back came chicken livers. But there was still a need to find another permanent item or two to add to the Big Three at all the restaurants. After much experimentation, it appears lobster tail will remain a constant as part of a "Benihana Special." Calamari steak (squid) also has a chance of being permanent. Whatever new items are selected, they will probably be in the seafood line—some kind of solid white fish that can be prepared in Benihana's filleted fashion.

Rocky is convinced, also, that sushi is part of Benihana's future. Ironically, one of the first campaigns Simoes created for Benihana was one that concentrated on the Americanized nature of the fare— "No icky, slimy things at Benihana" promised the ad. And that was absolutely right for the times. Now the times say something different. People like fish and people like fresh, and sushi gives you both. And it's trendy to boot. It was never difficult to convince Rocky to go to sushi because, despite his reputation as a sultan of steak, he prefers sushi to almost anything else. "If my sushi bars didn't make a cent, I'd still have them," says Rocky, "because I love to sit there and eat it."

With competition for sushi chefs as hot as competition for computer geniuses in this country, the best way to get a good one is to steal one from the competition, and Rocky has always been fond of this particular form of legalized larceny. "It might be what I like best about doing business in America," he says. "I can buy brains and talent." Not long ago a well-heeled couple sat at the sushi bar at the Benihana restaurant in Miami Beach and proclaimed: "We've eaten sushi all over the world and there's no doubt that your guy here is the best." The chef was one whom Rocky had plucked from a sushi restaurant in Manhattan. Rocky also has sushi bars in both of his Atlanta locations and in Anaheim, and there will be one in a new Benihana opening in 1985 in Lombard, Illinois. Late last year Rocky put together a deal for a Rocky Aoki Sushi Palace in Studio 54, the New York City discotheque, and there are plans for several more. There is still plenty of room for someone to come in and really grab the sushi market, and don't bet it won't be Rocky. "Some people think sushi has peaked, but I think it's just beginning," says Karas. "People in New York City might fly around from one sushi bar to another, but I'm not so sure people in Detroit or Oregon know so much about sushi. And I know Rocky knows that." "Yes," says Rocky, "I do."

Demonstrating his unusual talent for turning tragedy into triumph, Rocky even benefitted in the long run from his worst business move—the turning over of the managing of his company to Hardwicke. When the four-year association finally ended in 1980, Rocky had incurred a huge bank debt of about $5 million—the money he needed to pay off Hardwicke. The debt was not only cutting into profits but was also slowing down expansion. And existing as it did at almost 110 percent of the prime rate—Benihana was paying off the loan at rates as high as 20 percent—it was irritating as hell. Rocky needed cash.

Rocky could have made millions years earlier with a public sale of stock, yet he resisted. The reasons should be obvious. He is selfish. He doesn't like to share. He likes to call the shots. He did not want to be beholden to his stockholders, some of whom would have no doubt been less than thrilled to commit Benihana monies to a thirty-seven-foot powerboat or a trans-Pacific balloon flight from which the company's main asset might not return. But the bank debt was choking him, so in May 1983 the Benihana National Corporation was formed. Under its umbrella are fourteen of the existing and all future Benihana restaurants in the United States, three other new concept restaurants, contracts to do assorted Benihana-related items, and the new frozen food line. The stock began trading at about $5 a share and early in 1985 was ranging between $18 and $19. It was a sound business decision, and Rocky didn't exactly surrender the reins of power—he owns about 60 percent of the stock (2½ million shares were issued, of which Rocky has 1 million and Benihana of Tokyo has 1½ million) to go with his 100 percent control of the parent corporation. There are degrees of accountability, and in the business world Rocky Aoki is not terribly far from free agency.

The most interesting of the concept restaurants is called Big Splash: a Seafood Emporium, which was scheduled to open in North Miami

Beach in mid-1985. Its genesis serves as an ideal example of Rocky's business mind. While visiting Malaysia a few years ago he happened upon a combination market-open-air eatery. Customers selected their fare from vendors, then took it to cooks to be prepared. Rocky's mind started working. He had an idea. Now he had to—in the best American style—turn it into a concept. Rocky doesn't take a lot of meetings or lunches to figure out his concepts, though. Ideas race through his head on a nonstop basis, and there's no way of exactly telling how or when they take their final form. But one day Rocky envisioned a whole restaurant based on the Malaysian market concept.

It wasn't a totally new idea. There have been chain steakhouses that brand the customer's name on the piece of beef he chooses. There have been restaurants at which diners choose their own live lobster from a tank. When you think about it, the idea isn't too far removed from salad bars, which have become pervasive from New York to Los Angeles. But Rocky's idea was a little different and came along at exactly the right time. "He's doing like a food court idea only in one place," says Karas.

Once he had the idea, Rocky's Miami staff developed the whole restaurant within a few months. A site was chosen close to headquarters so it could be carefully monitored; given his druthers, Rocky might've preferred to open the first Big Splash in, say, Bora Bora, but things are done a little more scientifically these days. There is a solid bloc of year-round residents, but there is also plenty of tourism. Near the North Miami site are other Aokian outlets—Benihana restaurants in Miami Beach and Fort Lauderdale, and a Benihana fast-food outlet called Teri-yaki USA in the community of Aventura. And if Big Splash would for some reason fail to make one, it would be a very simple matter for Rocky to spend a few days in Miami and generate some publicity.

At Big Splash, the customer will have a wide assortment of fresh fish (perhaps some fifty kinds) to select from, some of it swimming live in tanks, some of it fresh on ice. A restaurant with such an approach has an overwhelming psychological advantage, says Karas. "There's a place called 'John Dominis' in Hawaii, where you walk in over a bridge over a pond and you see thousands of fish swimming along and you have the feeling, 'God, this is going to be so fresh.' Now, you really don't know if there's another stream in the kitchen bringing the fish back out, but it doesn't matter. You feel good about it." At Big Splash, the customer can feel even better because he takes his own fish to one of several cooking stations. The customer can eat in or take out, get the fish broiled or fried, spicy or nonspicy. It was a logical extension for Benihana. "We were one of the first restaurants to get the customers involved through watching the chefs," said Rocky. "Now they can feel even more connected to the process." In an Aoki restaurant of the future, perhaps, the diner will don chef's hat and apron and cook the meal himself.

So, Rocky took an idea and modified it to American terms. What was a basically small, peasant-type market and eatery in Malaysia became a 12,000-square-foot restaurant with a center serving area (to accommodate traffic flow) in Miami. What was an open-air establishment in Malaysia became a series of waterfalls, ponds, and fish tanks in Miami. It now bore the Aoki stamp.

But even more promising in the Benihana grand plan is the frozen-food line, a collection of main-dish entrees called Benihana's Famous Restaurant Classics. At the end of 1984, the line was established in about fifty major markets, and was a success in all of them. Total sales were estimated at about $40 million.

Typically, the frozen-food line owes its success to a holy triad of promotional assault, tenacity, and luck. Benihana spent nearly $1 million in advertising to launch the product in the New York area, and at least half that much in each of the Los Angeles, Chicago, Miami, and San Francisco markets. Rocky did several of the television spots himself, and also hired James Coco, a well-regarded actor and gourmet who has authored cookbooks.

The tenacity part came from Rocky's and his staff's unwillingness to miss out completely on what could generally be called the fast-food market. No matter how hard Rocky tried, his many and varied fast-food outlets over the years—Teriyaki USA, Chop-Chop, Oriental Express, Shanghai Express, Noodle Time—have not caught on. In point of fact, neither have anyone else's. The same American palate that seems to crave fast-food fried hamburgers does not care for quickie Oriental fare. So the frozen-food market was the next step up. And not an easy step. Benihana spent about $400,000 in research and development to come up with the *cyropacks*—frozen plastic pouches that are dropped in boiling water for a few minutes. They're good, too. Not as good as fresh food, but good. "I wouldn't have done the spots if I didn't think they were excellent," said Coco.

And the luck came in the form of timing. "It was superb," said Karas. "He hit the market at about the same time as Stouffer's and Lean Cuisine and some of the others, and he provided diversity. And because of the freshness and quality of Benihana, and because of the fact that there was no ethnic entree of substance in that market, he jumped into a wide-open category. Incredible. The restaurant helps the frozen food, and the frozen food will help the restaurant."

The frozen-food line characterizes the direction of Rocky's business empire over the next decade—a much slower expansion in number of Benihana restaurants and a growing dependency on long-range, carefully plotted product lines.

"Over the next ten years I see more Benihanas in secondary markets," says Joel Schwartz, president of BNC. "I see maybe twelve frozen-food items instead of the current eight. I see canned goods like Mandarin oranges, canned nuts, sauces, things like that. I see maybe a venture into Benihana active sportswear. Who better to push active sportswear than a guy like Rocky?"

"Now is the time to sell our brand name," says Tad Suga, who runs Benihana International Trading. "There is a whole untapped market out there for things like the teppanyaki grill. We are known for it. Why shouldn't we sell it?"

At the same time, though, the Benihana restaurants must remain at the center of the empire. With only the few exceptions, they've shown a remarkable resiliency over twenty-one years, considering that the average restaurant's life span is about ten years. The consensus within the company and without is that Benihana must continue to tap the secondary market, opening one or two restaurants a year in locales where it could still be an event. There is some movement within the company—primarily from Kobiyashi—to divide Benihana into classes. There would be a fancy class with a *prix fixe* dinner set at $25 or $30; maybe two chefs instead of just one would work each table. The second class would be the current style—medium-range prices, showy chefs, fairly diversified menu. The final class would remove the chef at the table and put a less skilled cook back in the kitchen. The result would be a cheaper meal and, according to Kobayashi, a means of rescuing New Orleans, Salt Lake City, and Cherry Hill from the financial doldrums. "I think one of our problems now is that when a customer goes in one Benihana and gets a free cup of coffee, he has to get it at another," says Kobayashi, "even if it may not be financially sound for one restaurant to be doing it. By dividing the Benihana system into three classes, you'd know exactly what you'd be getting and what you'd pay for it."

But whatever new plans are set or not set in motion, Rocky and everyone else agree that the basic Benihana concept must remain for the chain to continue to prosper. An outsider, Karas, defines it this way:

"The basic thing Rocky has to sell is freshness. The aroma and sensitivity of food. As long as he keeps selling those basics, he'll be ahead of the game. You know why? Because, basically, a lot of people don't trust kitchens. They don't know if something was made three, four hours before they got there. Now, I've not been to every kitchen in America, but I'll bet that somewhere along the line they all have to do some advance preparation. But at Benihana it's right there in front of you."

Rocky knows what he has to do, and he knows what pace he has to do it at. But that doesn't mean he's happy about it.

"We used to open eight, nine restaurants a year, but now that's impossible. Material costs have doubled; construction costs have doubled and sometimes tripled. Instead of spending a half-million for start-up, we're spending a million, two million. Look, starting a restaurant is simple. It scares a lot of people but it never scared me. It's not a big deal like people might think. But only if you have the money.

"It frustrates me. It really does. I still think of America as the land of opportunity, the land where you can do almost anything. When I can't do it, it gets me upset."

It truly does. A person who knows Rocky only from newspaper clippings about his exploits in the boat or balloon might get the idea that business really doesn't matter to him, that he could forget about it in a minute if he could fully occupy his time with daredevilism. But nothing could be further from the truth.

Rocky is about business. That is the thing that should never be forgotten about him, though it often is. By and large all the hobbies have gone by the wayside, and he could have left his business by the wayside, too, if playing full time is what he really wanted to do. Remember backgammon? He didn't give it up until "it started interfering with my business." He could have franchised the hell out of his restaurants in the early days and used the money to powerboat his life away. He could have gone for a huge, multimillion-dollar public sale anywhere along the line and ballooned his life away. He could have sold out to ITT or Hilton or any of the other giant conglomerates that offered to buy him out and begun, say, an ice cream empire in Hong Kong. But he didn't. He stayed in business because he loves the business of business, the acquisitions, the challenge of making money, of staying on top, of beating back all those other teppanyaki tables.

Business covers every facet of his life. Not long ago he was the subject of a six-part series in *Yomiuri Times*, a Japanese-language daily newspaper that has the largest circulation in the world. Someone else would spend the day counting the superlatives that were written about them. Not Rocky. He spent the day calibrating the effect, in sales, that the series would have on his and his brothers' restaurants in Japan. Likewise, a 1978 appearance on Merv Griffin's syndicated television show pleased Rocky only to the extent that "sales that week went up $300,000." Hey, he liked you, Merv, it's just that he liked what you could do for him more. Journalists are invariably impressed by Rocky's friendliness and candor, but what they usually miss is Rocky's motivation. Sure, he is by nature friendly and outgoing, but they shouldn't think for a minute that Rocky has anything else on his mind except the free promotion that the journalist can give to a Benihana restaurant. That is the legacy of Clementine Paddleford.

Pamela's penchant for astrology serves as another example of his constant business orientation. Her reader has said that down the road Rocky is going to make a fortune on real estate and oil. He agrees wholeheartedly. But when it comes to following Pam's AVAT warnings against traveling, Rocky shows astrology the way out. "I believe it when I want to," he says.

Rocky works all the time. "It's not like he brings business problems home," says Pamela Aoki, "because there's simply no separation." He's on the phone all hours of the night, making and accepting calls. He can be home for days without his path crossing Pam's, partly because of the size of the house, but mostly because he'll simply live in his office, stealing a nap on the couch when he needs it. He has a talent for catnapping that should be bottled and sold. If he decides there's nothing he wants to read on an airplane, for example, he can be asleep before the no smoking sign goes off. And Pam sometimes feels as if he may as well be asleep even when he is not. "He doesn't *hear* me half the time. For years I honestly thought he had a hearing problem. After his last operation for the accident in Florida he had a hearing test. I went and asked the doctor, 'Well, how bad is it?' 'It's fine,' he said. 'No problem.' It dawned on me that he didn't hear me because he was tuning in on something else."

"Rocky gets very uncomfortable and very restless if he's not making progress on something," says Pierre de Lespinois. "Small talk doesn't do much for him. Even when he's totally relaxed and seemingly enjoying himself, there's a deal going on."

Whatever subject Rocky is on at a present moment, chances are he's connecting it to his business. In that respect, then, he truly never spends an idle moment unless he's asleep. Pam sees the same thing that Chizuru saw twenty years ago when he took her to a war movie and equated it with the battle for restaurant survival. "We'll be in a restaurant and I'm thinking about what food to order," says Pam. "But Rocky is looking at the menu and getting an idea from it. Or we'll be window-shopping and he'll see some little specialty item that he knows would sell over in Japan. It can be very exhausting being with this kind of person, but it's interesting. Very interesting. I guess it's good in a way. There's not that many hours in the day, and he's got to be able to draw from his environment."

And his environment is everywhere and anywhere. The world of periodicals, for example. Rocky reads as many as anybody—*Time, Newsweek, Business Week, Inc., Venture, Success,* and *Fortune* are only a partial list. But he's not reading them for enjoyment or for edification of any kind other than to improve his business. "I'm looking for an idea I can use," says Rocky. "Period. I cannot read an article unrelated to my business. I cannot read an article just for the hell of it. I want to learn something I can use from it." Therefore, he doesn't read books, other than an occasional biography of a business figure (and that he will only peruse). "A book takes time, and only a little way into it I don't have any reason to want to finish it." He has already stated that he will not read this book.

There are two ways to look at that. Obviously, there is a whole literary dimension that Rocky is missing. One would not be able to sit around the bar at Benihana and engage him in a conversation about, say, Faulkner. On the other hand, he picks up an incredible amount of information from the things he does choose to read. To say that he relates what he reads to business is *not* to say that he reads only business articles. Maybe there's a new movie opening for which he could hold a premiere party at Benihana in Los Angeles. Maybe there's a new fashion trend that he could utilize for Benihana action wear. Maybe there's an onion surplus somewhere that would help him cut costs. The key thing to remember is that Rocky's definition of *business-related* does not stop where another businessman's might.

The eternal synergizing of environment to business requires a lot of discipline and a lot of time. Rocky even plays tricks on himself to make sure the process happens. One is to write a monthly column for a Japanese magazine *(Hoseki)* called "The Rocky Aoki Report." Rocky describes it as "a mixture of sports, business, sex, sort of an *Esquire*-type thing." He certainly doesn't do it for the money—it pays only a couple hundred dollars. And he doesn't do it because he loves writing. "In fact, I hate it. It is very hard for me." He has forgotten many Japanese words, and there is much about the English language that he has never known, and the result is a kind of mixed-up Esperanto, which he painstakingly writes out in longhand. "They change a lot back at the office," he says with a smile. But the point is, that type of endeavor for a nonprofessional requires an incredible expenditure of time and discipline to complete, yet Rocky does it because he feels it will keep him sharp. "It forces me to find out what's in, what's out, what's hot, what's not."

The biggest mistake someone can make about Rocky is to underestimate his skill as a businessman, or moreover, to underestimate the importance of business to his own definition of self. You can take all the things he's ever been—husband, father, collector, professional challenger, athlete—and there has been only one constant in his life. That is business. He was born to be a businessman, and in all likelihood, he will die doing business.

Though Rocky has obviously spent more time away from his desk than your average corporate chieftain, it would have been impossible to build and, more to the point, sustain a business as successful as Benihana with a part-time mentality. Yes, the time he has spent away from the restaurant in mad pursuit of another mountain-top has been an issue within the company, but the people who know Rocky best know that he simply has more hours to give than the normal person, even the nose-to-the-grindstone businessman.

"It's been a standard comment for a long time that Rocky's got to stop playing and get back to the business of business," says Simoes. "Well, you can argue that and argue that, but any objective observer would have to say he's done pretty well doing it the way he's done it."

"Truthfully, it's hard for me to say where the business stops and my own pleasure begins," says Rocky. "Sometimes I don't know myself. Let's take powerboat racing. It cost Benihana $800,000 a year some years. Now, if I did it all for myself, I have no right to ask them to pay. But the problem is for those people who want to know how it helped business there is no exact answer. Advertising is always like that. You cannot always tell what is getting customers into the restaurant. You cannot tell how many people found out about Benihana and came into the restaurant because of my racing. But even if I got Benihana's investment back and more, I can't say my driving was all for the business, no."

Obviously, Rocky's business style is almost impossible to define by conventional terms. It can only be described. Outwardly, he is light-years from the stereotypical business-only American. He can have fun with his business. It is not a deadly serious matter. He jokes about not eating at Benihana because "the food's too greasy." He'll gladly try other restaurants, even those of his competition, and he'll heartily praise the food if it's so deserving. One afternoon as he lunched at an Italian restaurant located downstairs from one of his own restaurants in New York City, he found a foreign particle in his seafood salad. Another man might have taken the occasion to criticize the other restaurant, or at least to launch into a sermon about the cleanliness of his own establishment, but Rocky just laughed. "Probably came from the place upstairs, no?" he said as a horrified maître d' came running over.

Yet, because his business style is not "Western" in the textbook sense does not mean that it is "Eastern." In fact, that style is probably further from being purely Japanese than it is from being Wharton-School-of-Economics American.

"Very simply," says Glen Simoes, "if his style were Japanese, we'd all have a job for life. That's not the case. He's very American in that he fires people; people come and go. Rocky doesn't know, through book learning, the methods of running a company, but he's an extremely quick study. He's a Western businessman only in that he's definitely not an Eastern businessman."

Yes, Rocky, the man who's quick with a smile and a good-natured quip, can fire people. He doesn't like to—and on many occasions he'll get someone to do it for him—but he'll do it. Within the last year he fired the advertising agency with which he and Simoes had worked closely for several years, and he fired an extremely close friend whom he had promoted through the ranks to the level of district manager. "He didn't do a good job so it was time we said goodbye," said Rocky. "Somehow he found out ahead of time that I was going to do it. He called me up and said, 'Rocky, are you going to fire me?' I said, 'Yes, I am.' Basically, I'm a nice guy but nice guys cannot win."

To all his employees, even the domestic help in his New Jersey home, he is known as a demanding man. Sometimes, he cuts through that toughness with humor, as when he walks into a near-empty Benihana in the middle of the afternoon, points to a bartender leafing through a magazine and says, "Not a bad way to make a living, no?" But if you work for Rocky, you'd better be working; it could almost be considered his one phobia, "I want to get my money's worth out of my employees. I feel I pay them *every* minute, *every* second that they're at work. I have to run my business that way." But he's not hung up on busy work. "What he looks for most is new ideas," says Bill Susha. "I'd say he's most critical of his executives when they don't come up with original thoughts."

Similarly, Rocky has a remarkably unsentimental view of what his employees think of him. Another man in Rocky's position might feel that his reputation as a dashing international daredevil would thrill a prospect into signing up at Benihana. But that is not Rocky's thinking. "People stay with me, first of all, because they make money. In Japan that is not the reason employees stay, but this is not Japan. In this country money is the main reason. People who work for me, like everybody else, are always looking to go elsewhere. The grass is always greener."

In truth, Rocky might not be giving himself enough credit. "Part of the attraction, a big part, of working at Benihana comes from

Rocky," says Simoes, who has been aboard for fourteen years. "It's his charisma, that wanting to belong to the winning formula that he has created. If you are selfish then, yes, your thoughts and his thoughts are going to rub, and you may not stay with him long. But he gives everybody a climate for self-performance and growth.

"I'm sitting on a three-million-dollar budget, and I don't think Rocky knows where the majority of it is going, nor should he. But I've got to accept that when he has complaints, he lets them be known. That's the way he works." Rocky elaborates on that. "Glen, basically, does what he wants to do, but we may talk or have meetings as much as three times a week. Hopefully, he knows more than I do about his line of work. I am buying his brain, right?"

Rocky simply does not *act* like other Japanese businessmen, either. "I've dealt with a lot of other Japanese, and you always do business with two or three of them," says Federico Vignati, Rocky's old back-gammon rival. "Then, after they consider everything, they'll give you a very polite reply. But when you deal with Rocky, you deal with Rocky. He may take time to study the proposal, or he may tell you yes or no right away." With Japanese businessmen, the exchanging of business cards (which are called *meishi*) is akin to a ritual act. A Japanese will bow, shake hands, and very formally present his card. Rocky? "I don't have cards," he says. "These Japanese guys are always bowing and handing me their card, and I have to say, 'Sorry, I don't carry one.' And they always say, 'Oh, that's okay. We know you.'" He's the exception that makes the rule.

If Rocky had a purely Western business style, however, the corporate structure of Benihana of Tokyo, Inc., wouldn't look like it does. "Yes, we're a little thin at the top," understates Simoes. "Thin" is not the word; "dissipated" might be. At a corporation the scope of Benihana's there are usually levels of vice-presidents and executive vice-presidents and senior vice-presidents, all reporting to somebody else in a chain of command leading to the chairman of the board. At Benihana, there are Rocky and four vice-presidents. Period. At one point several years ago the VPs decided they needed an organizational chart, just like the ones at conventionally run companies. But when they tried to draw one, they found so many gaps and slots unfilled that they scrapped the idea.

But the less formalized Benihana structure can produce more fruit, too. Decisions are not bogged down in committee or by a futile discussion of whose area what acquisition is under. The lines are clearly drawn and all of them lead to Rocky, whose word is final, except, of course, in the public subsidiary.

"I'd say we have a corporate combination here," says Joel Schwartz. "The American side of it comes from people like myself and Tony Carvalho, our treasurer, who came from traditional corporate backgrounds. The other side is Rocky, the intense loyalty his employees feel for him and the way he does things. It's a change for me and I like it. Take Big Splash. Rocky goes to Malaysia, comes back, and tells me about it, we get it centered with operations and boom, it's off the ground. Believe me, it doesn't work like that every place."

Much of the time Rocky isn't present at meetings in Miami, but he's kept abreast of all the big decisions that have to be made. When he is in attendance, the meeting might take on a more charged atmosphere. Rocky tends to want to do things at meetings, and usually what he wants to do involves an outlay of cash. There has literally *never* been a time, say his colleagues, when Rocky has been more conservative, less willing to plunge ahead on a project of some sort, than the other VPs. Their argument is always the same: "Rocky, it's your money. It's your company."

Though no formal poll has ever been taken, it's likely that most American corporate chieftains, self-made men or up-through-the-ranks gray suits, admire Rocky the businessman. Americans tend to like their mavericks, be they Bret, Bart, or Hiroaki. To the Japanese businessman, however, Rocky might represent something else.

"I'd say a handful of the Japanese admire him and relate to him very well for his ability to do the things he wants to do," says Simoes. "Most of the others resent him terribly. They think he's a little on the crazy side. Grudgingly, they might give him his due that he made it and deserves to be wealthy, but they wouldn't want their sons to be like him. They resent him because he didn't go through the ranks or fit the pattern. They look at him as less than honorable."

"I meet Japanese restaurant owners all the time who criticize Rocky behind his back," says Look, the former Benihana architect. "I say, 'Listen, if not for Benihana and the advertising and promotion they did, it would've been another ten, twenty years before any of you would have made it. Until Benihana came along, nobody knew anything about Japanese restaurants. It's because of Rocky that you people are in business. And they just shrug their shoulders."

"Some of the resentment of Japanese people toward him is because of jealousy," says Pierre de Lespinois. "He broke the mode of their cultural system and did it well. One of the most important things in Japanese culture is not to lose face, and Rocky has taken on a tremendous number of tasks that could cause him to lose face, to become dishonored by saying something and not being able to complete it. But Rocky's done what he says he's going to do."

Which brings him in step with perhaps the most important quality a Japanese businessman can possess—*giri ninjo*. The term is not easy to translate into English. Aki Sato, a Japanese businessman and a friend of Rocky's, spent at least thirty minutes one day consulting Japanese-American dictionaries and calling friends to get an exact translation. Suffice to say that it has to do with honor, charity, and integrity, doing things *correctly*. Rocky does this. Yes, he'll play the cutthroat game of business, but he never goes beyond the unwritten rules. More to the point, he loses with grace; possibly no one has ever lost with more grace than Rocky Aoki. "Unlike a lot of guys, Rocky sends the money in," is the way Simoes puts it. He "sends the money in"—it's a great phrase. His checks don't bounce, and neither do his relationships with his competitors. He'll beat you smiling, and he'll still be smiling when you beat him.

Rocky is not a con artist. He may look the part, but he's not. He's made good deals in his day—starting out with the acquisition of The Bamboo House twenty-one years ago, of course—but he doesn't use conniving and back-stabbing to complete them. That is *giri ninjo*. For his speech to the Junior Chamber of Commerce group on Kyushu, for example, Rocky was paid $30,000, plus first-class traveling and lodging expenses for himself and Pam. A decent haul by anyone's standards. Rocky thought so, too. So he convinced the group to add an extra session so more people could hear him talk. And he spent about one third of his $30,000 fee on an elaborate slide and video tape show. "I wanted them to get their money's worth," he says. That is *giri ninjo*.

Now, Rocky doesn't always get *giri ninjo* in return. (The Hardwicke deal comes to mind.) But Rocky doesn't have time to spend on revenge. The gentleman who introduced him to the Hardwicke people, for example, also got Rocky involved in a losing stock deal. But Rocky still takes his phone calls and still sits down to talk when he drops by Benihana. Pam Aoki says that equanimity has something to do with Rocky's spiritual side, which she discusses in the final chapter of this book. But it also has quite a lot to do with his business side. Almost every personal relationship Rocky has is colored by his business sense. Yes, his instinct is to want to be liked—there's not many of us who aren't in that camp—but he automatically transfers that to his business.

"I like to stay close to people, and one big reason is public relations," says Rocky frankly. "The National Restaurant Association says that one satisfied customer brings in seven hundred customers a year. People who meet me usually like me, and they'll remember that I treated them nice. They don't have to come back tomorrow, or this year, or next year, but eventually they will. Someone will say: 'Hey, let's eat at Benihana. I met Rocky Aoki and he's a nice guy.' And when they come back, I'll be here."

It would be fascinating to see how the Japanese business community would take to Rocky if he were in Japan wheeling and dealing on a more frequent basis. It could happen. Mama-san still works eight hours a day in the office and sometimes entertains business-related people at night. But she's seventy now, and she'd like nothing more than to have her first-born calling the shots. A talented calligraphist, Katsu recently won a prize in an art contest, and she'd like to spend more time on her avocation. Rocky has mixed feelings about becoming president and chairman of the board of Benihana Limited. He figures he'd have to be in Japan at least seven or eight times a year (as compared to once or twice these days) and that's a fourteen-hour trip each time with accompanying jet lag. To cut down on the time and the lag, Rocky might have to move to Los Angeles.

But on the other hand, the proposition is intriguing. The business already boasts a chain of twenty-five restaurants in almost every area of Japan. There is a lot more variety, too. One of the ironic consequences of Rocky's success in America is that it popularized teppanyaki cooking in Japan to the point that it was prohibitive for Benihana to get into that line. One of its restaurants, called Benihana of New York, is very similar to the ones in America, but the rest are Italian, French, or continental style. To capitalize on Rocky's fame, Benihana Limited recently opened a restaurant called Rocky's American Style. Predictably, it is doing very well and may soon be an entire chain itself.

Certainly, Rocky would expand the number of restaurants in the chain. And he would also have his eye on Europe. For years he's gotten franchise requests from businessmen in London, Düsseldorf, and several other cities. He's turned them all down. But from a base in Asia, he would be in much better position to monitor a European business. Most interesting of all for Rocky is the family land around Chiba, site of the present Benihana Ranch. Rocky's father paid about $150,000 for it fifteen years ago. Then the railroad came through near the land, and now it's worth about $16 million and rising. But Rocky doesn't want to sell. He's got several ideas for developing the land, ideas apart from the restaurant business.

As of December 1984, Rocky hadn't decided whether or not to accept his mother's offer. If he does, then the only certainty is that Japan will be buzzing in a way it never has before. The staid seniority system will be in serious peril. "Why did I come to work for Rocky?" says Joel Schwartz, who left a safe corporate position to come to Benihana. "Because it's never dull. With Rocky around, there are never any endings, only new beginnings."

# CHAPTER 14

As 1984 came to a close, Rocky was involved in a project that could take him 3,000 feet underwater—deeper than any human has ever gone—in a two-man submersible craft. The project is quintessential Rocky. It's expensive—the submersible is costing about $3.5 million to build, and another $1.5 million, at minimum, will be needed for expenses. It's dangerous—"Physically, it wouldn't be as taxing for Rocky and his legs," says Pierre de Lespinois, who is involved in the project with him, "but then again you're 3,000 feet deep in an acrylic sphere that nobody has ever tried before with tons of pressure." And it's complicated—there are territorial water agreements to be honored, technology to be created, financial sources (ranging from JVC to American public television stations) to be tapped. But the best guess is that it will come to pass. "If I don't do it, I'm going to be a liar," says Rocky, "so I must do it." Remember the old Japanese fear of losing face?

There are those who say that the submersible project would be Rocky's crowning achievement, his paean to immortality as it were.

It is highly risky, yet scientifically significant. "I think Rocky's getting to the point where he wants to leave something of significance," said a colleague close to the submersible project. "I think this is it."

That sounds good, but it's a misreading of Rocky. He is excited by it, challenged by the project as a whole—the scrambling for financing, the hunt for the proper publicity and then the voyage itself—but he is hardly possessed by it. "I hope to get maybe twelve good shows out of it," says Rocky, "but I'm not looking to be another Rocky Cousteau." And he's not. Though Rocky invariably affixes his personal signature to every project with which he's involved, he doesn't particularly care if the signature is rubbed off when he's through with it. Glen Simoes has seen this more clearly than anyone.

"I asked him once: 'Rocky, where do you want to be five years from now? I'll help you get there.' And he says, very honestly, 'Glen, I don't know where I want to be tomorrow.' He doesn't care for legacies or how people remember or respect him. His answer to all that is, 'Frankly, I don't give a damn.' And he doesn't."

The attitude accounts for the ceaseless ambition to push on, to look for something else and let the past simply lie. The one past obsession he seems unable to separate himself from is the boat racing—now and again the subject will come up in the Aoki household and Pamela will study him with a look best described as disgusted awe—"It's the one thing I really don't think he should do," she says—yet the sport doesn't paralyze him with preoccupation. Actually, what he regrets most is that he did not get a chance to drive the new fifty-foot crafts that represent the cutting edge of technology in that field; in other words he was not able to satiate his *imamekashi,* his passion for the newest thing.

In November 1983 Rocky was invited to serve as honorary chairman of the World Offshore Powerboat Association World Championships in Key West. He had a faraway look in his eyes one day as he surveyed the dockside scene: the huge, glistening machines, the mechanics and drivers scuttling about to prepare themselves for the race, the feel of competition in the air.

"I guess you wish you were out there, huh, Rock?" someone asked him, putting his arm around Rocky's shoulder.

The expected reply was a heavy sigh or a nod of the head with pursed lips, or perhaps an emphatic "you bet." But that wasn't Rocky's answer.

"Yes and no. I want to try some of these new boats because I haven't tried them. That's the only reason. But the rest of this? [His hand sweeps the area.] It's in my past."

He continues to look out into the ocean. Another idea is forming. Rocky's companion is reminded of a story a colleague of Rocky's told about Rocky's legendary restlessness. Rocky and this man had just missed a flight to Los Angeles, and there was Rocky studying the departure board. "My only question was, Where will he decide to go instead of waiting for the next flight to L.A.?" said the man. The answer was Honolulu. "We got to L.A. three days later." Rocky had that "L.A. in three days" look in his eye as he stared into the ocean.

"Maybe my dream is to win the America's Cup for Japan," he says after a long silence. "They go crazy over there for the sport, and I'm one of the few guys who can do it for them. It costs a lot of money and who wants to spend it? Who? You can count them on your fingers."

The idea seems, at first examination, even more outlandish than most of Rocky's ideas. A man with no experience in yachting buying a boat and going on to captain—needless to say, Rocky would also captain the vessel—his mother country to a victory in a sport that was for over a century the private domain of the United States. It took Australia that long to break that stranglehold, yet Rocky wants to do it soon.

But, then, it's not out of the question, is it? Consider, first, Rocky's desire to "do it for them." Lately, he's been feeling more and more

Japanese, more and more of a kinship to his heritage. It might be a normal consequence of growing older, of wanting to reach out and touch his roots before they wither up and die. But there's a practical consideration, too, as there usually is with Rocky.

"Japan has become a top country," says Rocky. "I am proud of it. They have money. They make quality products. Their economy is stable. They made something of themselves."

Rocky's ultimate accolade: "They made something of themselves." There is a strong motivation for Rocky to get back in touch with his country, and the America's Cup could do it for him.

Rocky still insists that his ceaseless ambition is a search to find something—his Holy Grail if you will—that will make him happy. "I am a very unhappy person because nothing satisfies me. Happiness is only for a very short period of time, when I make more money or when I buy something I like. But it doesn't last."

Neither do, for the most part, true friends. One who has, however, is Flip Wilson. Their relationship is an oddly synergistic one that doesn't seem to make sense unless you see the common ground on which the Black comedian and the Asian businessman have chosen to walk. Rocky doesn't even begin to analyze the bond between them; the comedian, rarely at a loss for words on any subject, has trouble explaining it, too. The best way to understand what Wilson really feels about Rocky is to hear him deliver, extemporaneously, two monologues involving Japanese characters, one of them a World War II soldier, the other a restaurateur named, not surprisingly, Benihana. Beyond the Japanese diction and phrasing, which Wilson captures precisely, is the nature of the characters themselves. They are gentle and kind, but not pushovers; they're light-hearted but not silly, "deep" if you will. The soldier is particularly revealing. In Flip's sketch he meets up with a Black American GI. They share sake and jazz and talk about women, all the while promising to pretend to be the other's prisoner should a commanding officer happen by. Gradually, they come to realize they would give their life for each other. Obviously, Flip has put a little of himself and a little of Rocky into those imaginary woods.

Flip feels that from the beginning there was something providential about his relationship with Rocky and Benihana. He first visited a Benihana in the late '60s when he was arguably the number-one comic personality in the country. He took Mary Wilson and Florence Ballard (the "other" members of the Supremes) to Benihana West in New York City for lunch and had a wonderful time joking with the other patrons. One of them was a stockbroker who gave Flip an inside tip. Almost as an afterthought, Flip went out and bought ten shares of the stock the next day. "I don't even remember what stock it was," says Flip, "but it was about 50 bucks a share. And what I DO remember is that I sold it for $5,700 one week later."

Shortly after that Flip and Rocky met through a mutual acquaintance, Paul Cooper of Atlantic Records. Flip told Rocky that Benihana had been lucky for him and, jokingly, added that he was going to eat at every Benihana in every city to pick up more good luck. "I travel a lot," said Flip. "I think I can do it." "No, you won't," Rocky answered. "I'm going to be opening restaurants faster than you'll be traveling."

Rocky was right—Flip never made it to all of them—but he did appear at literally dozens of Benihana openings all around the country. Rocky never asked him, and most of the time Flip didn't even tell him he was coming. But when the doors opened, there would be Flip, joking, jiving, and "Geraldine-ing" with everyone in the place.

In retrospect, what Flip did for Rocky at a time when his star was high as any in the comedic galaxy borders on the extraordinary. He received no money for his appearances—indeed, the subject never even came up between them. During his frequent talk show appearances, Flip would often spend as much time talking about Rocky and Benihana as he would promoting his own prime-time network show; Rocky remembers being embarrassed one day as he viewed John Davidson trying futilely to get Flip off the subject of Benihana. On Flip's right arm is a tattoo that says in impeccable Japanese script: "Rocky Aoki: Love, honor and respect, brother to brother." (Ironically, Rocky was both flattered and chagrined by it. In Japan only underworld characters, "Mafia guys" in Rocky parlance, get tattoos; Rocky couldn't get that out of his mind even though he appreciated the great compliment Flip was paying him.) On another occasion Flip passed on the Bing Crosby Pro-Am golf tournament, four days of sun, fun, and ego gratification at Pebble Beach, to fly 3,000 miles into a blizzard to speak briefly at a testimonial for Rocky in New York City.

Even today, fifteen years into their relationship, Flip has a hard time explaining exactly why he feels such a bond with Rocky. But what he does say throws light on the appeal of Rocky as a man who straddles two worlds, two codes, and two cultures.

It's late morning in Wilson's Malibu home. He's eating a piece of fried fish and listening to the Pacific Ocean crashing in his backyard.

"The funny thing about Rocky and me is that we rarely talk when we're not in each other's company. We rarely call each other up or write letters. We don't have to. He's my best friend in the whole world. Why?"

He stops to ponder the thought.

"I'll tell you why. Because he's an honest man. I don't know how much more simply I can put it than that. He's an honest man. How do I know he's an honest man? I'm not sure of that, either. Call it vibes. Call it the man's presence. I can't explain it.

"I guess our relationship has something to do with the culture Rocky comes from. I like the concept of honor. Death before dishonor."

Rocky and Flip, in fact, have an almost medieval (in the good sense) relationship, one based upon unwritten codes of behavior.

Rocky would have never asked Flip to attend a Benihana opening; neither would he thank the comedian if he happened to lift the event from the commonplace to the exciting, as he frequently did. "It was enough for me to go somewhere and do something for my friend," says Flip. "That's how I saw it. That's how he saw it." There is an implicit pact of sharing between the men, a kind of whatever-is-mine-is-yours concept. "There are so many things he did for me that I never looked for or asked for," says Flip. "I got married [one of three] in a Benihana. In my kitchen [he leads his visitor into the kitchen] is a hibachi table from the first Benihana restaurant ever built. See these swords [he points to two samurai swords mounted in his living room]. It used to be just one. A guy gave one to me and one day when Rocky was here I told him maybe he should try and return it to the rightful family in Japan. Instead of doing that Rocky sends me one of *his* swords. He told me, 'It's not right that I have three and you have just one. Now we each have two.' I have to be careful around the man. If I happen to say, 'Hey, I like that watch,' the man is going to take it off and give it to me. I gotta try not to like anything he has. The only thing I can give him is my time and my creativity, and it's fun for me."

At the same time the Aoki-Wilson code says, "Give me my own space." They don't have to communicate verbally. There's never any awkwardness between them when they get together after a long time apart, either. "Now, how in the hell can we be best friends when we're rarely in each other's company?" asks Flip rhetorically. "Well, all we know is that it's nice when we are. That's what's important." There are aspects of each other's lives that the other should respect and not attempt to change. After Rocky's near-fatal accident in San Francisco, Glen Simoes asked Flip to intercede and convince Rocky to quit racing. Wilson remembers their exchange as if it were written in stone:

Flip: "Would you please not race again? We are brothers and I am asking you on that basis."

Rocky: "As my brother you cannot tell me not to race. As my brother you must enjoy the time we spend together. I cannot promise you I will not race again, but as your brother I promise there will always be a place for you in the boat. If you enjoy living with me, and you think you would like to die with me, too, there will be a place for you in the boat."

"You know, I thought about that and said, 'Okay, I want my place in the boat.'"

And Flip has taken it. He's been beside Rocky on several boating runs. He's flown with him in a hot-air balloon and in an ultralight craft. All were because of Rocky's urging Flip to discover a sense of adventure within himself. Just as Rocky could never put a price tag on what Flip gave him, so could Flip not underestimate what Rocky helped bring out in himself. In Flip's mind, it crystallizes into one moment. A few years ago Flip was admiring a striking photograph of the *Double Eagle V* soaring past Mount Fuji during the trans-Pacific flight. "That's magnificent!" said Flip. "I've got to get a copy of that picture!" "No you don't," answered Rocky. "Why should you have a picture of me flying past the biggest mountain in my country? You should have a picture of you flying past Mt. Kilimanjaro." It hasn't happened yet, but Flip is working on it.

"Maybe the most important thing is this," says Flip. "We never asked for anything from each other. All we give to each other is ourselves."

Indeed, that might be it. Rocky knows what usually happens with his close friends. "People who start out as a friend unrelated to business sooner or later turn out to have a deal for me," says Rocky. "Then our friendship is changed. I remember once I had a close friend for about a year. That's all we were—good friends. One day I meet him and he's got eight people—*eight*—waiting to see me. Stockbrokers, insurance men, sales guys. Everybody's got a deal."

Rocky does seem to collect an extraordinary number of hangers-on. "Parasites, I call them," says Wilson. "People who want things out of him. I know how it is. I'd have a lot, too, but I just cut if off at the pass." Rocky, on the other hand, is porous at the pass. Some of the hangers-on amuse him and some get on his nerves, but he is never cruel to them. He is simply not comfortable with the king-of-the-pack role played by rock stars and other personalities like, say, the old Ali.

"His friends know him as being generous and easy-going, and sometimes people take advantage of that," says Pam. "I see many times when they think they're pulling the wool over his eyes or getting away with something when in actuality he knows exactly what's going down. There are times when I say, 'Rocky, what are you doing? This guy's stealing from you or saying bad things about you.' And he'll say, 'Hey, I know exactly what he's doing.' And sure enough, because he's so good with them, they end up giving something back to him."

Well, he doesn't always get something back. But he does seem to have a knack to come out on top of the relationship. He may get "taken" for some money, as he did in the Hardwicke deal, but he rarely gets "taken" as a human being. But Rocky goes on. Last year the Hardwicke guy offered to cut Rocky in on another deal. "No thanks," said Rocky. But he still takes his phone calls. Then there was his erstwhile mechanic, who, believing Rocky about to expire from his injuries in the San Francisco boat crash, started unloading his almost invaluable fleet of vintage automobiles. When Rocky found out, he didn't press charges. As the year ended, he was still engaged in some kind of settlement with the unfortunate man.

"I truly believe Rocky is a very spiritual person," says his wife. "You see it in the way he feels about people, the way he can forgive. He doesn't take the time out to practice religion seriously, but the spirituality is evident in his dealings with people."

"See, Rocky thinks in the long run," says Pierre de Lespinois. "Who will be better off in the long run, the mechanic or Rocky? The mechanic will never be trusted again, and Rocky knows that. As far as the act of larceny goes, Rocky can understand it. Money doesn't mean anything to him outside of it being freedom. Rocky has, or once had, a love of expensive cars. He can understand this guy. He can relate to him on that level. So he's not hung up on a lot of ideas of revenge. It doesn't matter anything to him."

They are similar points. And sound ones. But neither does Rocky go out of his way to cultivate close friendships. He is friendly, warm, open, and forgiving to everyone, which is not the same as selecting a few kindred spirits and getting close to them. There are several men at his income and success level with whom he feels a kinship, yet Rocky does not go out of his way to make them his confidantes. "See, I'm better off with people on my income level because I know they don't want anything," he says. "But people like that tend not to have many close friends. They tend to be business-oriented. I like it that way."

Rocky is not unhappy because he has no close friends. If there's such a thing as a friendly, gregarious lone wolf then Rocky would qualify. But there probably isn't.

"Speaking honestly, I just don't read Rocky as unhappy," says his wife. "He likes to promote and to be in the public eye and to create this kind of aura about him. He's gone through all sorts of different images he's presented to the public, and when this one came along, this guy searching for happiness, he said, 'Oh, this is a good one.' It gets people's curiosity up. It's interesting. How can a guy with all he has still be unhappy? Now, he would never acknowledge it because he's his own best press agent."

No, he does not acknowledge it. "Pam really doesn't understand it," says Rocky. "I am looking for more, always more."

Perhaps Rocky doesn't understand it himself. Another way to look at what he calls malaise and what Pamela and others call a good public relations front is that Rocky is running to stay a few steps *ahead* of unhappiness. He is not unhappy now, but he knows that if he stops for a moment—if the deals and the spiels don't keep coming—then he *will* be unhappy. Like the great white shark, he will die if he doesn't keep moving forward, and in that knowledge comes at least a part of the unhappiness he says he feels.

"I hope Rocky never reaches all his goals," says de Lespinois, "because I think it would kill him."

Surely, the man does not sit around in the manner of James Joyce and ponder his unhappiness. To see Rocky during the course of an average day is to see a busy man, and to see a busy Rocky is to see a happy man. When he ponders his unhappiness is anybody's guess. A typical day in the life of Rocky last year looked like this:

He arose at 6 a.m. in his house in Tenafly and started making phone calls. By 8 a.m. he had also received about a half dozen. As is the case with many businessmen, the phone could be likened to Rocky's respirator, breathing life into him. Rocky has a great standard line he uses when the caller says it's "important." "Important for who?" he says, "important for you or important for me?" Usually, it's the former—someone requesting a deal of what he calls the "ROM" variety. "That's 'Rocky's Own Money,'" he says. "The best kind of deals for me are 'OPM' deals—'Other People's Money.' But I don't hear many of them."

At 9 a.m. two visitors are shown into the house. They wear dark suits and no-nonsense expressions. "Ah, I'd like you to meet my tax shelter guys," says Rocky. The men wince and go on to explain how what they do can't really be called selling shelters but, rather, "looking after the investor's whole future" and "making careful, calculated investments." Anyway, after they're gone, Rocky says, "No matter what they say, they're tax shelter guys." And Rocky makes them very happy tax shelter guys by buying an $80,000 interest in an Arizona shopping mall.

Rocky chooses his Ferrari over the Mercedes limo, and we depart for Long Island City. As he motors along East River Drive near the Triborough Bridge, one begins to see how his mind works.

"Look at this, look at this," he says, pointing to the water as we drive along. "Look at what?" I say. "Look at how they're wasting the waterfront area. New York City is terrible that way. They lack ideas. They should have a marina here. They should have a small airport. They could make a fortune. I'm a water-oriented person. Things happen on the water. There's excitement, a sense of something going on. New York doesn't have that excitement anymore, and here it is wasting all this valuable water.

"The night before, I went to Bob Guccione's house to see about making some kind of deal for a Penthouse Club. It would be different from the Playboy Clubs. Playboy Clubs are not doing so well, did you know that? You know why? Things never change in there. The same kind of costumes, the same kind of high heels, the same kind of everything. People get tired of the same thing. You cannot survive having the same thing over and over for twenty years."

Just then Rocky spies an empty billboard with a phone number. "Copy that number down," says Rocky, who is busy guiding the car through heavy traffic. "This is a great spot for Benihana advertisement. Maybe 100,000 cars pass through here quickly." See a billboard, make a deal.

We arrive at the waterfront property he has been called to inspect for a possible deal. It includes a restaurant, a huge, dilapidated warehouse, and the potential for a marina. The restaurant is nice, but the warehouse appears ideally suited for a remake of *Night of the Living Dead,* and the marina potential seems just that—potential. Aoki sees something else. He gazes upon the ugly warehouse, spreads his arms wide and exclaims, "Beautiful! Beautiful! I have an idea for this." Eventually, though, he decides on North Miami for his first Big Splash.

Rocky leaves the waterfront and drives back over the bridge to Manhattan, stopping along the way to say hello to Mike O'Shea of the Sports Training Institute. While Rocky talks to the physical therapists who helped put him back together again, O'Shea remembered when Rocky first started training in the mid-1970s.

"A lot of the New York Knicks were training here then, and Rocky used to get in a little competition with them on who had the bigger Rolls-Royce. One day Rocky would come in a huge one, and the next day a guy from the Knicks would have an even bigger one. It seemed that Rocky always got the last laugh. Like the day he strolled in here with Marilyn Chambers just to bust their chops." Chambers, aka the Ivory Snow girl, was (and still may be) a queen of pornographic films when she became a Benihana customer in New York. One day she met Rocky. The next day he agreed to put up the money to produce her debut album as a singer. This was back in the Broadway-play days when Rocky was throwing money at anything that moved. "There was never anything sexual between us," said Rocky. "We were just friends." Rocky eventually bailed out when he discovered that the record would be released by what he called a "Mafia-related company."

"I never wanted to get swallowed up by Rocky," continued O'Shea. "That's why I resisted his advances about STI. He's a little too much hype for me. But on the other hand Rocky gave me $20,000 a few years ago for an awards banquet for kids with juvenile diabetes who had completed a program here. There were no photos or anything. Just Rocky and the kids. There are two sides to that man. No, there are many sides."

Rocky jumps back in his car and heads for Benihana West on 56th Street. Along the way he parks the Ferrari in a seedy area of Times

Square and enters an even seedier Chinese quick-food place, emerging moments later with a stocky Japanese man he introduced jokingly as "Mike, my pah-sonal massage guy." Indeed, Mike Mito is a talented masseur and acupuncturist who relieved Rocky of a great deal of pain during his recovery from the San Francisco crash. Mike is a little short on change these days, and Rocky helps him find a few gigs whenever he can. Rocky does have a natural inclination toward helping his neighbor, but beyond that he seems to feel the responsibility to be a sort of freelance Don Corleone to the Japanese masses who harken to his doorstep. The difference is that Rocky asks nothing in return. A guy like Mike can't help Rocky that much, but Rocky genuinely likes him. They cuss at each other in Japanese and trade inside jokes, which Rocky then tries to explain. There is no sign of patronization in their relationship, either. Rocky makes a crack at Mike; Mike makes one back at Rocky. Mike is a bit of a drifter and a homosexual, yet if the president of Mitsubishi were to walk in Benihana at that moment, he would share the table with Mike. If they had to talk business, Rocky might eventually ask Mike to excuse them for a few minutes, but there would be no trace of a "you're not good enough for this group" attitude. Rocky is a true populist, and that accounts for much of his popularity.

Rocky asks the Benihana bartender if Pam has been in. He slaps his hand against his forehead when he gets the answer. "I forgot something," he says. What he forgot was to inform Pam that morning that he had granted a request from a Japanese society to hold a meeting at his home in Tenafly. Pam had been caught completely by surprise. Later she explained the scene:

"I had been working all day around the house. I mean, I looked like a mess and I turn the corner and there is this grand, elegant party sitting in my dining room. Fifteen beautifully dressed Japanese ladies and the next thing I know I'm being introduced to the president of this association and that association. He sets this thing up and doesn't even tell me. It was vintage Rocky."

Back at Benihana, Rocky worries for a moment about the reception he'll be getting from Pam that evening (it was chilly but not frigid) before he gets on the phone and begins launching plans for competing in the 1985 Cannonball Exposition, a seven-day "One Lap of America" race that begins and ends in Detroit. The format pits celebrity drivers racing against each other in expensive cars. Rocky spent about $60,000 refurbishing his 1959 Rolls-Royce to compete in the 1983 race. He hired a crew in Los Angeles to film his arrival in that city, the halfway point. Soon after the race began, the director got a call from Rocky. "Listen, we had a little trouble," Rocky told him. "How far did you get?" asked the man. "About five miles," said Rocky. For all the money he spent, Rocky's brake system was declared unfit for competition. That's about $12,000 per mile. "But I'll be back in '85," he promised. "We'll get ten miles, absolute minimum."

Rocky is already late for an appointment at Farkas Films Inc. downtown, where he is to pose for the still-shot ads for the frozen-food line. There is a general moan a few minutes later when Rocky says he wants to buy film for his own camera. He returns an hour later. "Thought you only had to go around the corner," someone says. "It was a big corner," Rocky says with a smile.

Rocky drives back uptown to The Palace, which was at that time still open. Another supplicant for Don Corleone Aoki—this time a young Japanese who worked for Benihana at one time and now wants Rocky to help him find a job at a hair salon. Rocky leaves and returns fifteen minutes later with a job for the man. "Make sure you don't screw it up," he tells him with a smile.

It's almost 10 p.m. when he heads home on the Palisades Parkway. He glances at a vehicle stalled alongside the road. "I've never seen a

Japanese-made car broken down on the highway," he says. He walks in his front door at 11 and the phone is ringing. It's for him. Pam sighs.

"When Rocky's home, it's completely different around here. When he's here for a few weeks, it kind of burns me out to the point that I'm actually looking forward to his next trip. The staff gets crazy when he's around, too. I can sense it. Then, suddenly, he leaves for Miami one morning and the phone stops ringing and there are no strange people around the house and the pace slows down and everybody gets their equilibrium back before the next onslaught."

Rocky says good night to his visitor. "If you want to come back tomorrow, we could meet in the city," he says. "I have an appointment there at nine." "I'll pass," says his visitor. As the visitor steps out the front door, the phone starts ringing.

An upset of epic proportions occurred in the summer of 1984 when Rocky took a full-fledged, official, unplug-your-brain vacation with his family at a farm on the outskirts of London. It was really the first time he was away from telephones and Telexes for twenty years. He arose early, organized breakfast (he didn't cook it; he just organized it), puttered around the farm, took bad family photographs, and drove around London in a rented minibus. "I was crazy by the time it was over," he says, "but I did it." "I think he's mellowing a little," says Pam. "Before, we, the kids and I, were like another department for him in the 'ever-growing empire.' That's changing."

But Pam knows he'll never change completely. He's too afraid of stasis, too preoccupied with moving forward. What makes Rocky run? Hard to tell. But he's not running toward something as much as he's trying to put distance between himself and something he's never seen—inactivity, complacency, boredom. He doesn't spend a lot of time psychoanalyzing himself, but he's discovered the only truth he has to know. And that is that he can't stand still.

It's futile to contemplate what Rocky will be doing in, say, the year 2000 when he'll be over sixty years old. But one scenario comes to mind. It will be his way of saying hello to the new century. The first bulletins will read like this:

Millionaire American restaurateur and adventurer Rocky Aoki landed on Mars today, assuring himself and his privately constructed prototypical one-man spacecraft a place in the history of space travel.

A smiling Aoki emerged from his shimmering yellow and black *Benihana* spacecraft and, limping slightly, planted an American flag into the planet's red dust surface. He went back inside, emerged with a Japanese flag, and implanted it.

He reappeared a third time with a smaller flag bearing red flowers emblematic of Aoki's own chain of hibachi-style restaurants.

"The way I figure it," Aoki said with a smile, pointing to the flag, "these Mars guys have to eat. And I just have to find a way to give them what they want."

# CHAPTER

15

Sometimes you're on an elevator descending so slowly that you don't even realize which direction you're going, or even whether you're moving at all. People are coming at you in secret ways, and sometimes they're the people closest to you, all those smiling Iagos with secret agendas. Or maybe someone's out there thinking more creatively than you. Or you're just plain bored or tired of fighting the battles every day, and you're starting to lose more than you win, starting to lose your edge.

Or maybe, just maybe, there's a sense of inevitability at play, an adherence to the universal principle that nothing wonderful lasts forever, even something so wonderful as a Japanese immigrant opening a restaurant that no one comes to until one day, out of the blue, somebody named Clementine Paddleford stops in and writes a positive review and now *everybody* wants to eat there, and the way that Americans think about restaurants is changed forever.

In retrospect, it's hard to isolate one single reason that the final two decades of Rocky Aoki's life—both personal and professional—did not match the raging success he had enjoyed from the opening of the first Benihana in 1964 through most of the eighties. But when you hear the conclusion to the multi-layered tale of Hiroaki Aoki, sing no sad songs for the man. He never seemed, for want of a better word, *dreary*. Yes, he had to abandon control of Benihana, and, yes, though he seemed to honestly believe he would live forever, he didn't even beat the actuarial tables. He died in 2008 at the age of sixty-nine from a toxic combination of hepatitis C, cirrhosis of the liver, diabetes, and pneumonia. His ending was pure Rocky. As you'll see, it was complicated. When he died, much of the spirit, creativity, and soy-scented success of the phenomenon he created disappeared with him.

To grasp what was going on with Rocky in the years that followed the original edition of *Making It in America*, a story that ended in the mid-eighties, let's select the random year of 1993. Benihana Corp. had been public for a decade by then with a board of directors, dividend-seeking stockholders, and many, many more cooks stirring the celebrated Benihana onion soup than in those innocent days of yore. Rocky's second marriage to Pamela Hilburger had ended in divorce two years earlier, and Rocky, no stranger to philandering, was more unmoored than usual. He had six children, three each with Chizuru Kobayashi (to whom he was married from 1964 to 1981) and Pam, and several years later another child born out of wedlock would come to light. Rocky did the dizzying math at one point and concluded that he had fathered a child with three different women around the same time, a triumph of stealth if nothing else.

Benihana was, at best, holding its own. While Rocky's restaurants had never been in a footrace with grab-and-go staples such as McDonald's and Burger King, upscale chains such as The Cheesecake Factory and Romano's Macaroni Grill had become more prevalent. So had competitors specializing in Asian flavors, such as Panda Express (born in 1983), BD's Mongolian Grill (1992), and a particularly formidable competitor, P.F. Chang's (1993). It wasn't Japanese, but American diners didn't make the distinction; they were all just *Asian*.

The Food Network came along in 1993, too. Over time it brought expertise—at least *perceived* expertise—to millions of Americans who suddenly thought of themselves as certified gourmands, Craig Claibornes taste-testing in every suburban kitchen and sticking up their noses at Benihana's teppanyaki fare that smelled of a bygone age. Suddenly into our living rooms came exotic iron chefs wielding oversized knives and filleting fluke live, going on and on about *kurage* and *uni*. Benihana's menu was never boring or unsophisticated. Rocky had initially resisted what he called "slimy fish," but he added sushi to the menu back in the eighties. Still, its bread-and-butter remained the tried-and-true triad of beef/chicken/shrimp, and both the Benihana fare and the chef sideshows became ripe for sneering. Benihana, which had been the first restaurant to give us a show, suddenly couldn't measure up. It was the small-town carnival overtaken by a three-ring circus.

Benihana still expanded but at a much slower rate than years earlier. Despite the seeming ease with which Rocky had opened restaurants in the sixties and seventies, it kept getting harder. "If I want to open a sushi bar, all I need is a simple kitchen and some sushi cases," says Kevin Aoki, the lone Rocky progeny who stayed in the restaurant business. "I could probably open it for a couple hundred thousand dollars. But to open a teppanyaki restaurant with the twenty hooded grills you need? All that additional space you need above you? And a whole mechanical system? That costs more like $3 million to open."

Rocky's struggles mounted as various Benihana side ventures, such as an upscale restaurant called Big Splash and a frozen-food line, siphoned off revenue. They were not disastrous ventures, but nothing that Benihana tried clicked to the degree of Rocky's original idea of communal seating and table-prepared food.

Within the company there had been a cultural shift, not seismic but insidiously steady. "As Benihana expanded it became more of a chain-type restaurant where you almost forgot it was Japanese," says Kevin. "You're still sitting around a table and there's the chicken and there's the soy sauce. But what was missing was all the design elements we used to have. When my father started, he brought all the Japanese carpenters over and filled the restaurant with Japanese culture." Nobody talked about the Chinese elements in a Chang's—they just devoured the crispy green beans and the lettuce wraps—but Benihana had been *designed* from birth to be a Japanese experience, and that aspect steadily dissipated.

As Japanese culture was replaced by corporate culture, Rocky didn't do what was needed to reverse the trend. "My dad was always focused more on marketing than operations," said Kevin with an obvious tone of understatement. More and more shares of stock were issued by a board trying to maximize profits, and Rocky's presence within the company became diluted. He once owned all of it. When it went public in 1982, he owned 51 percent, a controlling interest. By the mid-nineties his shares were down to 25 percent and would ultimately tumble to 12 percent.

If Benihana had more or less peaked by that look-in year of 1993, so had the story of Rocky the Adventurous Madman, his body having been broken down from his many misadventures. Several forays into the Cannonball Run in the late eighties and early nineties represented the last great "what-the-hell-is-Rocky-doing-now?" adventures. The final Cannonball Run appearance by an Aoki, in fact, was not made by Rocky but by son Steve, who performed at a Detroit-to-Denver

Cannonball in 2017, a delicious bit of circularity that Rocky would've no doubt appreciated.

That Cannonball Run was perfect for Rocky—dozens of heavily modified luxury cars tearing around the country in a race that pretty much depended on violating traffic regulations. Rocky turned them into family expeditions, with Kevin accompanying him on two of his final runs, in 1991 and 1992. Another son, Kyle, remembers his dad picking him up at school in a heavily modified stretch Corvette limo that hung so low it made scraping noises when he pulled into the parking spot. "'Dad, how about bringing the Jeep next time,' I used to tell him," says Kyle.

One year in the competition Rocky drove a twenty-four-foot 1986 Cadillac Fleetwood d'Bardia Brougham limo stocked with, in the account of one Chicago newspaper, "a built-in bed, refrigerator, freezer stocked with Benihana frozen dinners, microwave oven to heat them up, cappuccino maker, sink with hot and cold running water (and sprayer for shampoos), and hand towels embossed with each driver's initials."

Rocky had a blowout before that race began. Perhaps it was a signal of things to come.

In 1997, Rocky made a big mistake. Brought in for questioning by the SEC, which had another target in mind, Rocky, candid as ever, admitted to making a profit of $346,000 on Spectrum Information Technologies stock. "He opened up the whole can of worms on himself," says Kevin. "He got very bad advice from people close to him. For all he accomplished in business, my father could be very naïve." Daughter Devon adds, "My father's Achilles heel was being a bad judge of character."

Rocky was fined $500,000 and given three months' probation for insider trading, but that wasn't his biggest loss. In most states, convicted felons can't operate a liquor license, so in 1998 Rocky stepped down as chairman of Benihana, ceding his board seat to Kevin, and, to a great degree, bringing to an end the Rocky version of Benihana as the century turned.

At sixty-one, his health began to deteriorate. Rocky had long believed that he had gotten hepatitis from a blood transfusion related to his 1979 boating accident. His failing health, legal problems, business problems, and personal problems—including seven children with varying loyalties to him—were enough to beat a man down. Except Rocky never seemed beaten.

"When the legal matter came around it was a crushing blow to the people around him," says Kevin. "I thought, 'He's going to die in jail.' But he got by that with the deal he took, and, to my dad, it was just another chapter, you know? It was something that was *supposed* to happen. Some of his friends had worked against him, but he never spent much time on remorse. 'Let's go forward.' That was him."


In 2002 Rocky secretly married Keiko Ono, a Japanese businesswoman and former Miss Tokyo runner-up, and the family saga got even more complicated. Rocky installed Keiko as CEO of Benihana of Tokyo (BOT), a separate entity that represented Rocky's remaining 12 percent of Benihana Corp. To describe the relationship between Keiko and Rocky's children as *acrimonious* would give understatement a bad name. Arguments, accusations, changed wills, and lawsuits (at one point Rocky sued four of his children to have Keiko control a $50 million trust he had created for them) flew around like sizzling shrimp on the spatula of a Benihana chef. At this writing, the legal ramifications are still not straightened out and would take an additional thirty pages to explain.

Families can be messy and complicated, and those adjectives describe the Aokis more than most. Still, the kids have all made their way in the world, two of them leaving a global footprint like their dad. Steve is a celebrated figure in electronic music while Devon was an iconic model (the face of Versace when she was just sixteen) and an actress (*2 Fast 2 Furious*, *Sin City*, among others) before she decided to bow out of the spotlight and raise a family. Having those two as siblings has provided a reliable line to older brother Kevin who owns and operates his own mini-empire of ten restaurants. "First I was known as Rocky's son," he says. "Then I was Devon's brother. Now I'm Steve's brother." The point is: This is a family with strong personalities.

The moms are a huge factor in the family dynamics. The oldest children (Kevin, Steve, and Grace, now called Kana) feel much allegiance to their mother and Rocky's first wife, Chizuru. The next three (Kyle, Devon, and Echo) feel the same strong fidelity to Pamela, Rocky's second wife. Devon, in particular, feels that Pam is too often dismissed as "the mistress" since they had a child while Rocky was still married to Chizuru. (Chizuru and Pam first became "acquainted" as they hovered over Rocky's bedside after his near-fatal boat race in 1979.) "My mother nursed my father back to health," says Devon. "She's one of the strongest women I know."

The seventh child is Jennifer Aoki Crumb, the "nonmarital child" as she is described in Rocky's complicated will, and she has been more or less accepted into the nuclear family. Her mother has never been identified publicly.

Rocky darted in and out of the lives of his wives and children with varying degrees of interest. Steve mentioned in the foreword the "tough love" he got from his father, while Devon admits "I was always his big baby. He was gentle and sweet to me. I didn't get the tough, critical Rocky that the boys got."

One could sense that all of them wanted more of what Devon had. Yet they all tend to conjure up the moments when Rocky was around, not the times when he was gone. Kyle and Pam both recall a wheelchaired Rocky, recovering from the boat accident, racing around with Kyle in his lap. "He had all these pins running through his legs and ankles," remembers Kevin, "but he'd struggle up and get down on the floor to teach me backgammon." And as Steve expresses, their lives were full of "experiences," if not consistent fatherly love. "How many kids get to go to a Malcom Forbes gala with their father?" Kyle asks.

So it was, then, that Rocky's slow crawl toward death—the only thing he did slowly in his entire life—brought this sometimes-fractured family together. In the final weeks, his kids often gathered, aware always of a delicate balance as they danced around Keiko and grasped for those moments when Rocky was clear-headed and not deadened by morphine. Sometimes they crowded together on his bed to talk quietly. Sometimes he seemed to hear them, most of the time he didn't. A few of the kids have some version of Rocky, when he was still sentient, saying a variant of *I don't want to die. I have so much more to do.*

"I saw him clawing to stay with us," says Devon. "It was the first time I ever saw him cry when he realized that time was running out, and his family was slipping away."

Kevin, the one most invested in the restaurant business, says that Rocky, in one of his last clear moments, had a business message too. In a halting voice, he said, "Don't lose Benihana. Keep it in the family." He believed that Keiko could work with the children and continue to put an Aoki imprimatur on Benihana. That didn't happen.

However sad it was, Rocky's death could not be said to be unexpected. "My dad," said Devon, "used all his body to the max."

In 2012 Benihana was acquired for about $296 million by Angelo Gordon and Co., a privately held, New York City-based hedge fund. Rocky was four years dead when the deal went down. "You can be sure," says Kevin Aoki, "that my dad would not have sold to them."

Benihana can still accurately call itself the largest Japanese restaurant chain in the world, but its influence is slipping and so is Angelo Gordon and Co.'s interest in it. Most industry insiders believe that it will be sold off, and, at this writing, one of the suitors could be Kevin Aoki himself, CEO of the Aoki Group, which owns and operates ten high-volume restaurants—seven in Hawaii, two in Miami, and one in Las Vegas, which he co-owns with brother Steve. How satisfying it would be for another Aoki to own Benihana. Like Steve and all the other kids, Kevin never received one dime from his father, even though he was in the same business. "But I did use what I learned working at Benihana," he says.

Kevin named his restaurants with the past in mind. Indochine 38, for example, refers to the year of his father's birth; the *Bluetree* in Bluetree Café is *Aoki* translated into English. One of the most popular restaurants in his mini-chain is a remodeled version of an original Benihana established in 1971. Kevin has a simple name for it: Rocky's Teppanyaki, but most people just call it Rocky's. "When I'm inside it," says Kevin, "I feel my father's spirit."

In truth, the old Benihanas don't mean much to the family anymore, with the exception of Kevin, who lives in the restaurant world. But there are moments that stir the memories. Several months ago, as of this writing, Kyle Aoki visited his sister Devon's new home in Miami. Devon ordered takeout one night. From Benihana.

"It was delicious," says Kyle. "And it was the first time I had food from a Benihana since my father died."

*Left to right*, Kyle, Rocky, and Steve.

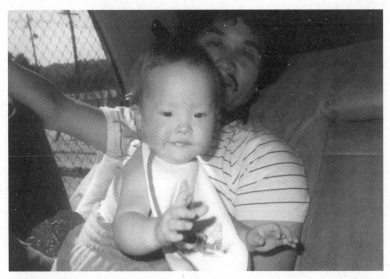

Rocky with Devon.

# EPILOGUE

Almost forty years after I spent several fascinating months with Rocky Aoki compiling the first edition of this book, I still remember lots of moments that make me smile, including powerboat races in Miami and balloon flights in Albuquerque. But one truly stands out. I was at the New York Athletic Club one afternoon interviewing some people who knew him. Rocky was an NYAC member, well aware that the discriminatory organization would not have allowed his membership a decade earlier and still might not have were he not rich or famous.

One of the members was gasbagging on and on about how I could not write or use anything that had not been cleared by NYAC members because normal freedom-of-the-press rules did not apply there. He had a theory that the NYAC had special rights granted by the government or the cosmos or somebody. Rocky, who had been working out, caught the last part of it as I was telling the guy he was full of . . . uh, that he was mistaken.

"Rocky, tell him," the guy said.

But Rocky turned the tables. "Hey," he said in a soft voice but with true passion. "This is America. Everybody can do what they want." The guy looked around for a hole to crawl into.

*This is America. Everybody can do what they want.* That in a nutshell was Rocky Aoki. He did not became a citizen until shortly before his death, he filled his restaurants with Japanese artifacts, he hired mostly Japanese workers (at least in the early years of Benihana), and he was never a flag-waving, lapel-pin-wearing bore who told you what a true patriot he was. But I'm sure I never met anyone who loved this country more than this Tokyo-born immigrant who didn't step foot in the States until he was twenty years old. It was that undying faith in America that led him to accomplish what he did.

Rocky and I didn't keep much in touch after I finished the initial edition of this book, then titled *Making It in America*, in 1985. I was busy and he was busier. We shared a quick lunch in New York City in the early nineties and we talked on landline phones a few times after that. Once I called him to ask for a restaurant recommendation for a trip I was taking to cover an NBA event in Tokyo. When we got to the restaurant, three friends and I discovered that the bill was pre-paid.

We fell out of touch, and I still regret it. To my surprise I found myself shedding a few tears when I read his obituary in 2008. Rocky had the ineffable quality of being supremely fun to be around. Not fun in the same way that it was to be around superstars such as Michael Jordan or Magic Johnson as you watched everyone in their vicinity genuflect and turn into jelly. Rocky's star wasn't in that stratosphere. And not fun in the sense of watching someone command a stage and essentially monopolize the scene with an unending monologue, the way Muhammad Ali or Charles Barkley did.

The fact that Rocky sometimes disappeared into the crowd is somewhat difficult to reconcile because everything about his life sounds outlandish, oversized, and outrageous. But Rocky the person—or *pah-son* as he put it in his heavily accented English—wasn't any of those things. When in large crowds, he tended to fade into the background, partly, perhaps, because of his diminutive size, but mostly because he just wasn't comfortable in big gatherings. His son Steve, who at his shows hurls cakes and is borne aloft through the audience on a raft, obviously got that comfortable-in-crowds personality. Rocky was better in small groups.

There was an authenticity about Rocky, a genuineness. The light fell upon him because of the things he *did*, not the things he *said* or the way he said them. Sure, he was a self-promoter. But the boats he drove and the balloons he co-piloted never had "Rocky" on them. They bled Benihana. He did not conduct his business in a Trumpian fashion. People came to know his name, but it was because *Benihana* dragged *Rocky* along with it, not vice versa.

His genuineness lent him a certain unguarded quality. Even many athletes I've covered who are considered outspoken are careful and even defensive about their image. Not Rocky. He harkened back to the boxing promoters of old whose motto was: *I don't care what you say, just say something.* And if he didn't like what you said, he not only didn't hold a grudge, he more likely didn't even remember it.

Our publishing agreement for *Making It in America* was defined from the outset as a biography, not a first-person autobiography. I would find out the information and write it the way I saw fit. Since I didn't have an expertise in business, the 1960s dining scene in New York City, Japanese history and culture, and a hundred other things, I needed to check almost everything with Rocky and/or his public relations ace, a smart man named Glen Simoes.

Rocky didn't pay that much attention to what I wrote—sometimes I wondered if he read the pre-submission excerpts at all—though Simoes kept a close eye on them and at one point, Pamela Hilburger, Rocky's wife from 1981 to 1991, objected to a few things that Rocky had revealed about their private life. I didn't blame her in the least. Rocky was asked to referee. Half-listening to both of us plead our cases and not sure what to say, he offered the following in his clipped Japanese accent that ignored some verbs and contractions: "Jack the writer. Maybe that his style." It's still a phrase used with humor in our household.

When Rocky was building his reputation there was no social media. Would he have been more guarded had his every comment been tweeted or Facebooked? When the reporting of one impolitic remark could damage a restaurant's rep? I honestly don't know, but I tend to think he would've been the same unguarded person. Had Instagram been around in the sixties and seventies when Rocky was building his empire, photos of Benihana would've blown it up. His social media staff would've been larger than his posse of table chefs.

Another aspect of Rocky's genuineness was his almost childlike affection for sport. Not sports. *Sport.* The idea of competition, mano a mano, figuring out a way to be better than the other guy, and then shaking the other guy's hand when he beat you. Rocky wasn't an all-for-one-one-for-all type of team guy though. It was his nature to embrace individual sports, to do it alone. His successes in wrestling, backgammon, and boat racing spoke to his thirst for individual competition, and I'm quite sure that, had he possessed the technical know-how to fly a hot-air balloon, he would've done it himself and not with a team.

Simoes used to say to me: "The key to unlocking Rocky's success is to figure out how he blended the Japanese part of him with the American part of him." I'm not sure I ever did figure it out aside from acknowledging that, yes, he was a creature of two cultures to be sure. As Steve put it, "True, he was the glitzy Americanized entrepreneur, but he was also the archetypal Japanese man, aware of manners, selfless, restrained, preoccupied with self-sustenance."

Who knows how many times in that first year of Benihana, all those nights when literally no one came into the restaurant, Rocky could've folded up and gone back to driving the ice cream truck in Harlem or, for a safer option, back to Tokyo, where he could've easily found a job, perhaps even worked for his father, despite the fact that they fought constantly? But that wasn't Rocky. He wasn't going to lose face. He was going to endure.

Rocky's decision not to help his children financially isn't exclusive to Japanese culture, of course, but it doesn't exactly skew American. In most cases we like to give money to our kids just to show we have it. He believed that you shouldn't give away money just because you can, not even to those closest to you. "He paid for all our education, and, obviously, we ate well," says son Kyle. "But aside from that he wasn't a gift giver."

Yet in his own way he was generous. Perhaps the most underrated aspect of Rocky as a Japanese man was the opportunity he gave to people in his native land. "My father brought thousands of Japanese immigrants into this country to work, and he treated them right," says Kevin Aoki. "Benihana was a safe place that they could come to. To this day people come up to me and say, 'I'm here because of your dad.' That makes me feel really good."

How is Rocky distinctly American, or, put another way, how is he different from the archetypal Japanese model? That would've been a more relevant question several decades ago before notable Japanese athletes such as baseball players Ichiro Suzuki, Shohei Ohtani, Yu Darvish, Hideki Matsui, and—I gulp as I say this—competitive eater Takeru Kobayashi became well-known in our culture, along with writer Haruki Murakami and the white-haired conductor Seiji Ozawa. Rocky and Seiji, by the way, shared a Manhattan apartment for a short while in the 1960s while they both struggled to get started. My guess is that their egos may have clashed. Rocky always said that Ozawa's music "give me headache," and there is no record of Ozawa chowing down on sesame chicken at a Benihana.

Ozawa, being in the arts, was expected to be different, but Rocky was an anomaly to corporate culture in Japan which was, and still is to a large extent, button-down. We know men like Kiichiro Toyoda and Soichiro Honda because of the iconic products they manufacture, not their inclination to climb into race cars or hot-air balloons. "My father used to tell us that, in Japan, they have a saying," says Kyle. "'The nail that sticks out gets hammered down.' Well, my father wasn't afraid to stick out." Kevin notes that the really successful Japanese men tend not to be entrepreneurs. "They are the CEO types. They're very, very successful, and their companies are famous. But they themselves aren't. The reason my father was such a hero in Japan for such a long time was that he was something new. He chose a different path."

That path changed the way Americans ate and thought about going out to dinner. Devon has talked to several chefs about Rocky—Nobuyuki "Nobu" Matsuhisa and Masaharu Morimoto being two of the most famous. "They both say how much my father inspired them," she says. Do we buy Devon's story, that two of the world's most innovative chefs say they were inspired by a man who had limited culinary chops himself? Well, I buy it. Innovators are invariably remembered and revered by those who follow, maybe even *especially* by those who surpass them.

At a time when Japanese cuisine was pretty much unknown in America, a time not even twenty years after we dropped atomic bombs that destroyed two major Japanese cities, Rocky Aoki not only brought us Japanese food but told us, "Hey, you'll enjoy sitting down and eating it with total strangers." We didn't believe it until we did it. His faith that people would eat together was a reflection of his ultimate faith in America.

Throughout the eighties and nineties, Rocky took a photo with everyone, it seemed, and so one can be found of him with Donald Trump, two masters of the universe, though we knew not how true that would later become. There is the tendency to put Rocky in that Trumpian tradition, at least identify him as an early iteration of the high-living Gothamite titan of business, endlessly promoting, endlessly womanizing. But I don't place Rocky there. He was too kind, too compassionate. Pam remembers their first date together. He showed up in a three-piece suit, in which he helped change a flat tire of an unfortunate motorist they encountered. Kyle remembers them walking in the city and encountering a homeless man who was screaming about a bug in his house. "So, my father went into the guy's cardboard shack, found a cockroach, and kicked it out," says Kyle. "'There,' he told the guy, 'it's safe now.'"

There's also a photo of Rocky with Richard Branson, well before he became *Sir* Richard. Devon remembers Branson calling to pick her father's brain. Rocky fits more comfortably in the Branson profile. The British-born magnate at least talks about matters beyond his bottom line and stamps VIRGIN, not his own name, onto everything.

Perhaps some kind of future Branson notion was kicking around in my head when I ended the original edition of *Making It in America* with a hypothetical anecdote about Rocky piloting a one-man spacecraft to Mars and planting the flags of America, Japan, and Benihana on its red soil. Rocky didn't have Branson money—and certainly not the resources of Jeff Bezos, another billionaire space explorer—but it would've been fun to see Rocky with those guys, endlessly dreaming, endlessly scheming, securing funds from somewhere to explore this new frontier. It's what he lived for in his adopted land because, in America, *everybody can do what they want.*

Except for what Rocky wanted most. To live forever.

# INDEX

# ABOUT THE AUTHOR

**J**ack McCallum was a writer for *Sports Illustrated* for thirty years, and is currently Special Contributor. He is the host of the break-out podcast *The Dream Team Tapes*, based on his *New York Times* bestselling book *Dream Team*, and is also the author of *Seven Seconds or Less* and many other titles. While concentrating mostly on basketball—in 2005, he won the Curt Gowdy Media Award from the Naismith Memorial Basketball Hall of Fame—he also edited the weekly Scorecard section of *Sports Illustrated*, covered five Olympic games, and has written about virtually every sport, including bowling, bicycle racing, squash, and wrestling. McCallum teaches journalism at Muhlenberg College and lives with his wife in Bethlehem, Pennsylvania.